How to Run a Marathon in 13 Years

How Hard Would You Fight for Your Dreams?

JP Mac

Cornerstone Media

Library of Congress: 1-11615934861

ISBN 13: 978-1-954278-10-3

Published by Cornerstone Media

La Cañada, California

10 9 8 7 6 5 4 3 2

Contents

THE LONG SLIDE   1

1. 2008   3

2. 2009   15

3. 2010   31

4. 2011   43

5. 2012   53

6. 2013   61

7. 2014   71

8. 2015   81

ASCENT   93

9. 2016   95

10. 2017   103

11. 2018   115

12. 2019   125

13. 2020   137

14. 2021   149

15. Old Ground   159

16. By a Thread   169

17. Starting Block   179

18. Loop One   187

19. Loop Two   195

20. Cool Down   205

Acknowledgments   211

Resources   213

About the Author   215

Also By JP Mac   217

About the Publisher   219

THE LONG SLIDE

Chapter One

2008

B est Picture: *No Country for Old Men*
Super Bowl Champ: New York Giants
Billboard Top Song: "Low" by Flo Rida
U.S. President: George W. Bush
Top Web Browser: Internet Explorer

> "Often, I do not know toward what I am running. Most of the time, I do not care. I cannot precisely see my goal, but I can talk about getting there."

— Hal Higdon

Sharp pain in the left knee.
I stopped and walked a minute, then tried running again.
But the sharp pain intensified.

Back to walking, I passed under the freeway, sipping Gatorade on a hot September morning. Above me, traffic rumbled on the 210 Freeway, flowing east to downtown Pasadena or west to La Cañada, with its expensive homes and yet more freeways. Two miles to the south lay the Rose Bowl and parking lot K. In K's northwest corner stood a small Coastal Live Oak tree: the finish line for my 18-mile run.

A slow jog brought more sharp-pain-in-the-left-knee, a condition I named SPITLK (pronounced spit-lick). More walking, then another running try, then spitlk. I wasn't too concerned. Aches and pains cling to distance runners like barnacles to a dock. Over the last several years I'd suffered a broken fifth metatarsal (foot bone), torn calf muscle, lateral meniscus sprain (damage to the outside knee cartilage), and assorted other fleshy dings.

I'd rocked the Eugene Marathon back in May. Now I was aiming for prestigious Boston. To enter America's oldest marathon, you must run a qualifying race within a specific time. For middle-aged me, that meant completing 26.2 miles in three hours and forty-five minutes. My qualifying race would be the California International Marathon (CIM). The entire summer I'd honed my race plan, cross-trained, and increased mileage. Come race day in December, I'd be primed.

For now, I'd hold off on running. Since walking produced no spitlk, I'd stroll the last two miles to Lot K. Why stress an unknown injury? Today I'd ice the left knee, rest, and ice on Monday, and resume training Tuesday.

But Monday brought unease. If I missed the CIM now, I'd miss Boston the following March. I needed a little medical reassurance. Off I drove to Pasadena to visit Doc Smith. A sports chiropractor, Doc Smith was around my age with a salt and pepper beard and a lean runner's build. He'd helped me recover from my meniscus sprain. In his office, I let him push and straighten and knead my left leg. I hoped there was no problem. I even spelled "no problem" out in my head.

Then Doc Smith frowned. "I'd get an x-ray."

"As a precaution, right? I mean, you don't see a problem, do you?"

"My guess is a bone bruise or a stress fracture."

"Doc, come on, I'm training for the CIM. This is my Boston shot."

"Hell of a time to happen. I sympathize, believe me, but your knee doesn't care. Get an x-ray."

Angry at Doc Smith, I left his office. I deserved a better diagnosis. I'd paid my race fee and already rented a hotel room. Several of my Team in Training teammates were driving up to Sacramento to cheer me on. I was ready physically and mentally to soar this year, not some 2009 date-to-be-named.

On the 134 freeway, I passed the creepy Colorado Street Bridge. With its old-school streetlamps, huge neoclassical arches, and numerous suicides, the bridge was said to be haunted. Parallel to the concrete Arroyo Seco Channel, the trails beneath the bridge were old training paths. I recalled running those paths. Passing beneath the Colorado Street Bridge, I'd always kept an eye out for spectral shapes or falling depressed people. With the bridge now solidly in my rearview mirror, I brightened. Okay. Fine. An x-ray would nail down this knee business.

Just then, my TV animation career was suffocating for lack of projects, dying like a frog in a sealed jar. I hadn't worked a union job in a while. No union work meant no sweet union medical benefits where the care was outstanding. My wife Joy and I were covered with a plan through my sub-chapter S corporation. Our health had been good, and we'd hardly used our insurance.

Thus, I was unprepared for medical bungling.

A week inched by before I could secure an appointment with a doctor. Because of his rapid medical assessments, I called the doctor assigned to me, Doc Jiffy Lube. After sitting forty-five minutes in a waiting room stuffed with patients, a nurse finally took my vitals. My blood pressure was excellent. I weighed 198 pounds. Then Doc Lube breezed in. Early 40s, with silver hair and well-manicured nails, he oozed competence and trust. Here was the face of medicine that would diagnose my knee.

Explaining spitlk, I pointed, gesticulated, and indicated. I managed to mention my six half-marathons and five marathons over the last three years. Doc Lube absorbed the information, nodded, placed both hands in the pockets of his crisp white coat, then said:

"You'll need an x-ray."

Another week passed before my left knee was x-rayed at a separate location. Then a third week slid by before I could snag a follow-up appointment with Doc Lube. I was still an assistant marathon coach with Team in Training—TNT—but it was frustrating. Thanks to spitlk, I hadn't been joining the team on our Saturday long runs. And the clock was ticking on my qualifying marathon. I needed to be locked in on my own training.

Back to Doc Lube's for the follow-up, I checked with the paperwork gals. Yes, my x-rays had been sent over from the separate location. Doctor Lube himself had initialed their receipt. In the examination room, Doc Lube was his usual brisk self:

"Stay off the knee until we get the x-rays back."

"Really? The front desk said they're here."

"It's not like anyone told me."

We walked to the front desk. Doc Lube avoided eye contact with the paperwork gals and checked my x-rays.

"Tendonitis. Rest. Ice the knee. You'll be fine."

"Wait a second, are you sure?"

But Doctor Lube was gone, delivering curt medical insight to the masses.

I fumed on the drive home. I'd need a new doctor, which was probably another three weeks of appointment-x-ray-follow-up. And I still had no good explanation for spitlk.

By now it was early October. My training schedule for a 3:45 finish was shot. Completing the California International Marathon seemed doubtful and qualifying for Boston was on the back burner.

Could I salvage something? Next month was the Pasadena Marathon. Most marathons offer lesser-distance races, like pilot fish trailing a big shark. I'd signed up for a half-marathon to test my race pace. Forget 8:35 a mile. Could I even finish 13.1 miles? Meanwhile, I'd already added a few pounds. Though no longer running 30-mile weeks, I still possessed a 30-mile-a-week appetite.

As the October weather cooled, my left knee turned coy. It was like living with a manic depressive. I never knew what would trigger spitlk. Sometimes at team practice I'd walk and jog several miles pain-free. I inserted walk breaks into my brief runs, jogging for a minute, then walking two minutes to relieve knee stress. Sometimes I'd be fine. Other times a short jog would ignite spitlk.

One Tuesday evening, I loped around a four-hundred-meter track for eight laps. No sensations at all. This had been my longest continuous run in almost two months. By now, CIM was a wash. That Sunday's half-marathon seemed doable. For a race plan, I'd run/walk, but mostly stroll, the Pasadena streets, like being in a parade without equestrian units.

Mother Nature objected.

Fires in Santa Barbara and Sylmar, coupled with off-shore winds, filled the Los Angeles basin with ash and smoke. The outdoors smelled like a vast ashtray. On the morning of the Pasadena Marathon, I woke early and got dressed. Before I could leave, a teammate called from the start line. Due to poor air quality, the marathon had been canceled. No seventh half-marathon for me. I was more depressed than the housing market.

Karla was a fellow Team in Training coach. On Saturdays, she worked with our walking participants. Her day job was nursing. I'd been updating Karla on my knee. She said that tendonitis is usually treated with anti-inflammatory medications. Had I been prescribed any? I said there was an excellent chance Doc Lube couldn't tell an anti-inflammatory from an anti-aircraft gun. I was still tangled in health care red tape, attempting to acquire a new doctor. RN Karla suggested that once things sorted themselves out, I ask for an MRI and learn the root causes of spitlk.

In the meantime, I experimented with something called chi running. Founded by a distance runner named Danny Dreyer, the form incorporated aspects of tai chi mindfulness and body alignment into a running form. In his book, Dreyer stated, "Chi running is all about setting up conditions that make running, easier, more efficient, and injury free. . . . most runners [run] upright with a long stride. They landed on their heels, feet out in front of their bodies. . . ." Danny Dreyer felt this style was the primary cause of running injuries. Heel striking overworked the legs by impacting ankles, shins, knees and hips as runners must pull themselves forward with each step.

A glance at my shoes told me I was a champion heel striker.

Rather than land on your heels, Danny Dreyer prescribed aligning the body in a precise manner, a column, then falling forward. Gravity, not leg strength, would propel you down the road. The feet now landed underneath the hips, center of gravity slightly ahead. You were in a controlled fall. Dreyer claimed that by maintaining the proper angle of lean, you'd glide along, focusing on relaxation and keeping your body moving as an upright column. Dreyer pointed out that "the lean is very slight, and each individual must find his or her own sweet spot."

It sounded like New Age gibberish. Did I need to run with a scented candle? While waiting for a new doctor, I studied Dreyer's book, practicing as best I could.

In addition, I took a lesson from a laid-back chi running instructor named Steve. In a park on the westside, myself and a half-dozen other seekers-of-new-running techniques tried absorbing Dreyer's method of locomotion.

Falling forward is a scary experience. Since childhood, I'd been taught to avoid crashing on my face. Except for a period of heavy drinking, I'd been largely successful. Now I was supposed to topple voluntarily. Every time I tried, my body tensed. Both feet would grip the ground like a cat sliding toward a river.

Steve introduced us rookies to intricacies such as aligning your body in a column, cadence, letting the hips drift back. Such times as I was able to run, I felt a bit of spitlk, but it was slight. Steve used a digital camera to videotape me standing still in chi posture, then transitioning into a run. He showed me where I'd lean enough to initiate the chi running but then quickly revert to overstriding and landing on my heels.

"Helps if you think of this as something that evolves," said Steve, "like practicing the piano or marriage."

Until my MRI, I figured to stick with chi running. Hopefully, my new doctor would order up an MRI, diagnose spitlk, toss in a little physical therapy, and I'd be back running again by spring at the latest.

Thanksgiving passed. As the country prepared for a new president, I finally canceled the California International Marathon. Disappointment is a harsh brew. However, the race officials were cool. They extended me credit. After I healed, I could run the race next year. What decent, kindly folk. But December '09 seemed a little late. I'd be up to marathon speed again by late summer.

Rains came, and the fires died down. Many Team in Training teammates departed to run the Honolulu Marathon. Next month, our winter season ended with the Phoenix Marathon. Despite my uncertain physical condition, I'd drive out and help coach. In the meantime, I'd shifted my limited training away from the Rose Bowl.

I'd been running the trails along the Arroyo Seco Channel south of the Rose Bowl. In some sections, they were rock-studded and hungry for limbs to twist. I had enough problems without an ankle injury. My other preferred trails were north beyond the bowl. If anything, those trails were even rockier. They led beneath the 210 freeway where I'd first met spitlk, up a steep hill, under Oak Grove Drive in Altadena, to the Devil's Gate Dam. From there, the trail crossed a brushy watershed, past the famed Jet Propulsion Laboratories, up a second steep hill, and into the Angeles National Forest. On up the trail climbed past a triangular-framed bridge to the Elmer Smith Bridge, five miles from Lot K. Our team tradition was to slap Elmer's metal sign, then turn around and run back.

But the hills produced excess spitlk. I sought flatter terrain.

Around the Wilson-Harding Golf Course in Griffith Park were bridle trails: soft dirt and a minimum of elevation. Perfect ground for a novice chi runner. I covered a few miles there three times a week. To be safe, I included one-minute run/two-minute walk ratios. One morning I trotted along for fifty minutes with only minor soreness and no spitlk. It felt like progress.

As the New Year approached, I was in pretty good spirits. Joy and I had downsized back in May, right before the real estate market cratered. We'd bought a condo and paid off our debts. As an editor for magazines as diverse as *Guns and Ammo* and *Bon Appetit*, Joy had seen her own career pancake as the internet devoured ad revenue, mortally wounding the publishing industry. But money from the house sale kept us solvent.

2009 would be better. We'd both find work and I'd qualify for Boston.

Chapter Two

2009

B est Picture: *Slumdog Millionaire*
Super Bowl Champ: Pittsburgh Steelers
Billboard Top Song: "Boom Boom Pow" by Black Eyed
Peas
U.S. President: Barack H. Obama
Top Web Browser: Internet Explorer

> "All you need in this life is ignorance and con-
> fidence, and then success is sure."

— Mark Twain

Around the 13-mile marker, a steel band struck up a
peppy version of "Brazil."

Moments later the pace convertible cruised past. Pas-
sengers sprawled against the seats as if recovering from

an all-night kegger. A few waved languidly to the sidewalk crowd. An open truck jammed with journalists and photographers trailed the pace car. They snapped and clicked and filmed a pack of hard-running East Africans.

I'd located the front of the marathon.

Tired after a poor night's sleep, I continued my coaching duties. First, I needed to find a particular Team in Training participant. TNT runners were easy to spot as they wore dark purple shirts with the name Team in Training, a chapter, such as Greater Los Angeles, names of various corporate sponsors, and a white space to print first names in magic marker. (These were very busy shirts.) TNT participants also tended to run in bunches like healthy grapes.

Heading down the sidewalk against the flow of the race, I passed families in lawn chairs with homemade signs: "We Love You" and "Keep Going!" The weather that Sunday lingered in the 50s, slowly growing warmer as the day matured. Because of holiday travel, the last several weeks I hadn't exercised much. But so far today, whenever I'd jogged, my left knee had cooperated. I felt hopeful. Had I outlasted spitlk?

Out on the course, the East Africans were followed by non-East African pros, then a few more elite runners, then three very fast men running together, then the lead pack of elite women. They, in turn, were chased by a handful of very fast women. Spread out after them came the merely fast non-elite men and women. And finally, the street filled from curb to curb with the balance of seven-thousand marathoners.

A red sign for the three-hour pace group rose above the runners. Clustered around a fit-looking man and his sign were those who wished to finish 26.2 miles in three hours. Behind that pacer flowed more pacers with their own signs as if in a bidding war—3:15, 3:30, on down to 5:30. I moved around the race, seeking my participant, scanning the race for purple.

In 2007, I'd been a Team in Training participant. Team in Training is a fundraising program for the Leukemia and Lymphoma Society. TNT participants are coached to run marathons, or bike a hundred miles, or run triathlons, all while raising money for blood cancer research. Many teammates, coaches, and captains had friends and parents, wives, or kids suffering from blood cancers. Or were survivors themselves. That January morning, I wasn't battling acute myeloid leukemia, non-Hodgkin lymphoma, or multiple myeloma. I was only trying to stay warm.

In the pre-dawn Valley of the Sun, the temperature lurked at a bleak 29 degrees Fahrenheit. Warm buses conveyed our team from our hotel to the start line. Coaches Kate and Katie forced a reluctant group of grapes to disembark into the frosty pre-dawn morning. A small line formed at gear check. There you'd turn in warm-up clothes such as jackets, sweatpants, and the like. Said garments would be trucked to the finish line for later reclamation. Shivering runners held onto their extra layer of clothes until the last possible moment.

I was among them, doing jumping jacks with my teammates near the massive anchor from the battleship *Arizona*. As the start time neared, we finally joined the gear-check line and shed our outer clothes. I kept on a frayed blue sweatshirt that covered my purple shirt. Rubbing my arms and legs, I entered the start corral for runners deemed capable of finishing in 4:30.

Walking in elliptical circles, I kept checking my watch as if waiting for a cab. I'd exhale and see a white puff of breath dissipate, reminding me of my grade school days and frigid winter mornings delivering newspapers in suburban Chicago.

Suddenly, the people ahead moved off in a choppy wave. I followed, happy to be in motion. About a mile and a half into the race, the sidewalks and gutters were covered in old sweaters and sweatshirts as if people were trying to keep the sidewalk warm. I added my blue sweatshirt to the piles. Later, the clothes would be scooped up, cleaned, and donated to charity.

At my first water stop, the paper cups were topped with a thin coat of ice. It was almost too cold to drink, and I wondered if I'd catch brain freeze. At the five-mile mark, a boy of around eleven cheered us on. Sprinting along the sidewalk, he cried, "Go, runners!" Then the kid stepped on a patch of icy concrete. Out went both feet, and he landed on his butt, more surprised than hurt.

Phoenix was billed as a flat fast course. Truer words were never uttered. With miles of ruler-straight city streets, there wasn't even symbolic elevation. That meant the absence of relief that rolling terrain supplies to overused muscle groups. In the latter miles, I'd walk backwards or sidestep during walk breaks, providing my legs, hips, and butt muscles a little change up.

I was employing a 5x1 run-walk ratio. That meant for every five minutes running, I'd walk a minute. Pioneered by former Olympian Jeff Galloway, run/walks were standard fare for us in the Greater Los Angeles, San Gabriel Valley Marathon Team. Participants who hadn't engaged in serious sports since high school freshman soccer could ease into long distances by running, then walking. Periodic walks reduced breathing and heart rate, allowing the body a little recovery, and helping mitigate fatigue in the taxing late miles of 26.2.

Gradually, the ice in the water cups melted. For a time, another teammate and I ran together as the day grudgingly warmed. We parted at mile 16, and I surged ahead. Slightly ahead of pace at mile 20, I smiled at Coach Kate, waiting to run me in.

In her late twenties, low-key Kate was lean, quiet on her feet, with several Boston finishes in the three-hour and thirty-minute range. I was in my mid-50s, 215 pounds, with a single marathon finish in a disappointing time.

Thirteen months, some hard training, and a broken fifth metatarsal later, I was in Phoenix, eager to exorcise the ghosts of my first marathon.

Through miles 20 to 22, Kate let me set the pace. We continued with the 5x1 run/walks. Come mile 23, my iliotibial bands hurt. The IT band is a tendon running down the outer thigh from pelvis to shin bone. It keeps hips and knees stable during running. Just then, my IT bands felt as flexible as bathroom tile.

Running ached less than walking and running, so I dropped the walks. Kate then took the lead. We picked up speed. A young woman from Mississippi ran with us briefly, grateful for the company. She fell behind as the racecourse entered an industrial area. Stark and dystopian, the surroundings appeared like a set for *The Walking Dead*. Hardly an onlooker anywhere—no cheers, no "you can do it." This was grit-your-teeth running of a brand I wouldn't sample again for a long time.

The road rose to accommodate a bridge over a canal. For the first time all morning, there was a rise in elevation. Like water sloshing in a bathtub, I felt the blood in my legs repositioning.

Atop the bridge waited our senior coach, Katie. A hard-charging, diminutive former college track runner, she waved us on. As we passed, she called out to Kate, "Pick up the pace. He doesn't look gassed."

I wanted to pick up Coach Katie and shake her like a daiquiri.

Descending the bridge, we rounded a curve. Crowds lined the road ahead. Spectators cheered. ("You're almost there.") Coach Kate said, "Coming up on 25."

"Yeah," I gasped.

She sped up, but I didn't follow.

Over her shoulder, Kate said, "John, I guess I'm a little surprised at you."

I sped up.

Blowing horns, whirling rattles, ringing bells, encouragement from the crowd. Good energy.

To distract from my IT bands and other assorted aches, I focused on orange traffic cones, staring at one until I passed, then locking eyes on the next, as if rubber cones exerted a mysterious pulling energy. I resented Kate and her crisp pace. We hit 26 miles, barreling into the last .2.

And there it was ahead: the finish line.

As we crossed the timing mat, Kate and I locked hands, grinning.

4:21:45.

Race personnel flashed me funny looks. Kate steered me to the medical tent. Apparently, my pasty face was even whiter than usual; unsurprising, since every spare drop of blood had pooled in my legs.

Sitting down on a cot, I felt light-headed. Both IT bands throbbed as if smacked with pipes. But inside I glowed like a star on the cusp of nova.

Not so much in January 2009.

Cutting the course in several spots, I reached the back of the marathon, locating my participant. A walker, friendly, and outgoing, Kim had a cackle like a Halloween witch. Loud and startling, her laugh was like having your neck grabbed from behind by an icy claw. My immediate task was to motivate Kim beyond the cutoff point. In big city races, there's usually a time deadline so streets can be reopened. Traffic cones and barriers are taken away and water stations removed. Miss the cutoff and you'll end up on the sidewalk, weaving around lawn chairs. In some races, you're directed off the course.

Joining Kim, I urged her to dial up the pace. Behind us, yellow lights spun as a street sweeper gobbled up discarded water cups like a monster Pac-Man. But Kim felt nature's call. I suggested she choose a toilet just past the cutoff point. But Kim couldn't wait and darted into the nearest john.

Waiting with one eye on the street sweeper, I heard Kim unleash a mighty cackle. Something pretty darn funny must've occurred. Strolling pedestrians leaped as if electrified. Clearly, they were in the presence of a haunted Porta-Potty.

Kim made the cutoff and entered the second half of the marathon. I headed back down 44th Street. Cutting through the pilot fish half-marathon, I made for the nearest light rail station. In Tempe, I hopped off near Sun Devil Stadium. There I took up a position at mile 25.

Same course as 2007, same finish line. As teammates came down off the bridge, I joined them. We'd run or walk to 26. With the finish line in sight, I'd peel off and jog back to 25 to escort another participant. I attempted chi running, but it ended up mixed with my old heel-pounding style. As the afternoon passed, the temperature rose into the 70s. No spitlk, but I was in poor condition. Fatigue whittled me down.

After steering in one of our participants, a cheery young singer and actor called Boston CJ, I folded. On a flat rock near the finish line, I slumped, scowling at the passing runners. I was disgusted with being so out-of-shape. I wished I were running the marathon. Kim was the last of the San Gabriel Marathon Team to pass. Whether she unleashed a celebratory cackle, I can't recall. Campaign Manager Tiffany and I rode the light rail back to our hotel. Plunging into a deep sleep, I missed the victory celebration.

Encouraged by a spitlk-free Phoenix, I decided to test my knee. Back in LA, I ran 2.5 miles up into the Angeles Forest. A homeless man, bearded like ZZ Top, watched me lope along. Among the trees, I passed an odd collapsed stone bridge. Overgrown with brush, the bridge sat crumbling, like a lost Mayan temple. Moving at a modest run/walk of one-minute running to two minutes walking,

I felt gratified at the absence of spitlk. Maybe I'd had tendonitis after all and the knee had healed. Later that day, I chronicled my experiences and blogged, "I'll slowly build up mileage to around 20–25 miles a week. Once there, I'll begin working on speed."

A day later, shifting furniture around the house, I awakened spitlk. What the hell? A week passed and I emerged from a swimming pool to again encounter spitlk. This didn't bode well. I'd finally gotten my health insurance to cough up another general practitioner. Hopefully, the new MD practiced a less haphazard form of medicine than Doctor Lube.

A gnome-like man, Doctor Minu's shoulders were hunched as if he'd spent years shrugging off matters beyond his control. He seemed patient and methodical. Minu heard my story, performed an examination, checked the x-rays, said nothing about tendonitis, then recommended an orthopedist.

During the ten days I waited for my appointment, I walked in Griffith Park. Since December, our house money had taken a hit. Both our Mac laptops were old. My car's mileage now topped 100k. Thus, we'd shelled out for two new laptops, a used Jeep, a trip north for the holidays, then a trip east for me to attend a wedding in Chicago.

Joy earned some money copyediting part-time. I'd finished up several non-union scripts last fall but hadn't worked since. In the TV animation field, networking should be woven into one's DNA. Before your current job ends, you need to be calling around, angling for the next gig. But I was a loner, fond of loner pursuits such as reading, running, and brooding over slights. During my years at Warner Bros., I could be funny and charming or sullen and hostile. No wonder my phone didn't ring. I wouldn't call me.

In February, I met with orthopedist Doctor Ang. Thin for a non-runner, I suspected he might be vegan or very sick. Ang examined, questioned, listened, and pondered. Finally, he said, "I'm going to recommend you for an MRI."

RN Karla would be pleased.

"Great," I said. "What's the plan?"

"I should look first at the MRI. Until then, no more running or walking or that running/walking, or that chi approach you mentioned."

"Nothing?"

"Just don't."

For once, I didn't.

On a rainy March evening, I arrived for my MRI.

"Choice of music?"

"Light classical."

An MRI technician placed headphones over my ears, that connected to a portable DVD player. Magnetic Resonance Indicator technology created 3D anatomical images by a complex process of magnetism which excited the protons found in the water of tissues. Any changes in the proton's direction were recorded. This allowed physicians to note the differences in various types of tissues. In my case, the tissues were in the left knee.

MRIs were loud, hence the music. I was slid into a device that looked like a huge egg roll. Magnetism was then loosed to do its stimulating work. I relaxed. This was progress. I believed the MRI results would eventually clear me to run another marathon. Maybe that fall.

In April, at the same Boston Marathon I once might've run, Ryan Hall finished third in 2:09:40. Kara Goucher took third among the women. Of the top ten male finishers, only Hall and fellow yank Timothy Cherigat were not East Africans. Around the same time, in the office of Dr. Ang, the slight physician deciphered my MRI.

Here is a recreation of our talk.

Dr. Ang: "You have damaged your left knee cartilage."

Me: "Wow. Bad?"

Dr. Ang: "Think of friction creating a pothole in the cartilage."

Me: "Okay, I will. What's next?"

Dr. Ang: "Often, such a pothole is plugged with cartilage taken from a cadaver."

Me: "Then I could run again?"

Dr. Ang: "If you were 18. Because of your age, we must debride the bone above the knee so that blood flows into the pothole. This will eventually build new cartilage called fibrocartilage."

Me: "Surgery, huh?"

Dr. Ang: "Arthroscopic, yes."

Me: "Okay, this is serious. Sounds like no marathons for a long time. Half a year?"

Doctor Ang sighed. "Fibrocartilage will be fine for many activities. But it is weaker than your original cartilage. It can't stand up to the strain of running, especially a marathon. You would destroy your knee."

My mind spun, searching for loopholes. "Shit."

Dr. Ang: "You can't run anymore."

On the day before the operation, I ran two miles. For the second mile, I dropped the run/walks and sped in, logging a 7:56. I hadn't run a mile that fast since last August. As the month of May ended, I felt pretty good. Doctor Ang was just playing it safe in case I trashed my knee and sued him.

Then surgery. I went into the hospital in the morning and came home that afternoon. Then I adjusted to having a big fat swollen knee. Accidentally torquing it brought intense pain. Crutches were necessary. Immobility did boost my writing production. While no animation work arrived, I was blogging on two sites and churning out short stories. None were selling, but I was cranking them out all the same.

By July I could swim and use the elliptical machine. Doctors Minu and Ang reminded me not to run. I asked them about chi running, falling forward, and no heel striking. They were unimpressed.

"This chi method doesn't matter," said Dr. Minu. "Don't run."

Doctor Ang was more specific. "Don't run anymore."

As a late athletic bloomer, I'd just gotten started with marathons. Now I'd lost the California International Marathon. I'd lost Boston. On top of that I was supposed to chuck out any future chance of seeing how far and fast I could run 26.2; maybe break three hours and thirty minutes one day, then keep going until my limitations said stop. Worse, the doctors wanted a lid on all running-jog-ging-shuffling. Period. There had to be a way: maybe chi running, maybe something else.

Glenn agreed.

Starting physical therapy, I was first examined by the head of the clinical team. Glenn was in his late twenties and competed in sprint triathlons. He surmised that the excessive stress on my knee originated with weak glutes (gluteus maximus—the butt muscle) as well as weak hips. Glenn understood my desire to run again. He hadn't heard of chi running but grasped the principles. Finally, a kin-dred soul.

Therapy continued twice a week through the summer. On September 7th, the Station Fire spewed a massive vol-cano-like pyro cumulus cloud over the Angeles National Forest. On the same day, I marked my one-year spitlk anniversary.

My de-potholed knee remained tender. Frustration comingled with a lingering sense that Minu and Ang were right: running was past tense like youth or steady employ-ment. Glenn recommended I lose weight and continue strengthening my left glutes and hips. He suggested walking thrice a week. At the first sign of spitlk, back off.

Physical therapy ended in October. I attempted walks on all-weather tracks plus the soft dirt of Griffith Park's bridle trails. About a mile was all I could cover per session, wary about summoning spitlk.

I missed Team in Training, the camaraderie, the encouragement, the positive vibes. Of course, I could always show up at practice. But observing everyone running felt depressing as if I were the Stasi officer in *The Lives of Others*.

In November, I walked around the track at a local high school. On the field, the marching band rehearsed under the leadership of a peevish band director with a bullhorn. The band had been given blue dots to mark their places. But the band director felt they weren't lining up correctly. *("Everyone get on their dots. Aaron, I said get on your dot. Now. Run. Okay. I can be a lot harder, if that's what you want.")*

To my surprise, the California International Marathon remembered me once again. Without asking, they extended my marathon credit another year to 2010. Such decent race people. Toward year's end, I could walk a spitlk-free 1.5 miles once or twice a week.

I'd try a brief run in January.

Chapter Three

2010

B est Picture: *The Hurt Locker*
Super Bowl Champ: New Orleans Saints
Billboard Top Song: "TiK ToK" by Ke$ha
U.S. President: Barack H. Obama
Top Web Browser: Internet Explorer

> "Run. Because zombies will eat the untrained
> ones first."

— *The Zombie Apocalypse Survival Guide.*

A shiny new decade opened before me.

Ten years earlier I'd been living in a big house in the hills above Los Angeles, employed by a major studio, and planning for Y2K societal collapse. Joy and I were recently married. Petersen Publishing employed her as assistant managing editor for *Hot Rod Bikes* and *Custom Classic Trucks*. I had also produced and directed a short film. But submitting it to numerous festivals proved fruitless. Only Florida's Space Coast Film Festival ever aired my wee opus. A minor hiccup; financially and professionally 1999–2000 were my zenith.

Save for a rogue 5k in '95, my running back then was infrequent. I'd jog two miles on the steep grades around my house. Occasionally, I'd drive over to the Rose Bowl for a three-mile jaunt. I smoked a lot, but other than a touch of arthritis, my health was solid. Everything seemed great, the future on track to remain golden.

To boost my athletic spirits in the new decade, I resolved to run a 5k that fall. For obscure reasons, I picked the Chapman University 5k down in Orange County. Slated for October, those 3.1 miles would signal my official return to racing. I had no reason to be confident, save the old saying that fortune favors the bold. All that remained was learning to run without screwing up my knee.

I could barely chi walk—forget running. By February, two miles was about all I could do. But something new appeared: a dull soreness in the left knee. Once again, I backed off walking, rested, and iced. Something in my chi walking method seemed screwy. So, I made another appointment with chi running instructor Steve.

Near the Rose Bowl Aquatic Center, Steve watched me chi walk, then chi run. Chi running relies on a steady cadence: both feet striking the ground so many times a minute in a sweet-spot range between 170 and 180 beats per minute—bpm. Faster foot turnover means less time supporting the body's weight on one leg and overall energy expended. Quick foot turnover equals a more efficient runner. To speed up in chi running, you lean forward. To speed up in chi walking, you increase bpm. A lot of moving parts to this chi locomotion.

Steve noticed I'd somehow mashed chi running and chi walking together. After sorting out my cadences and bpm, Steve said that running would return. When it did, he figured I could increase my cadence by one bpm a week. Say from 154 to 155. (Forget 170.) As mentioned, chi runners and walkers carried around little metronomes, peeping out their beats-per-minute. Like the alarm clock-eating crocodile in *Peter Pan*, you always knew when chi folk were around.

March arrived with another LA Marathon. Several TNT chums participated, including Coach Kate. My former pacer finished strong. Since Phoenix, Kate had celebrated a slew of firsts. In April last year, she'd run her first 50 miles with fellow TNT Coach Kiley at the Leona-Divide 50 Miler. Busy Kate had then married my first TNT coach, Jimmy. Having recently given birth to her first child, Kate's 3:23 finish was her first postpartum marathon.

As for myself, I managed to walk three miles in Griffith Park. Very hopeful. But I still couldn't run without spitlk.

Thanks to a Scooby-Doo script, I'd switched back to the Motion Picture Industry Health Plan. I scheduled a physical with my old general practitioner, Dr. Nakamura. A naval reserve officer and former marathoner, Nakamura and I had both run the Honolulu Marathon. Nakamura examined and tested, heard about my knee woes, checked out a painful right shoulder, and noticed an odd spot on my nose. He referred me to an orthopedist and a dermatologist. When all the medical smoke cleared, I'd found myself with a fresh trio of health maladies.

A bad tendon.

Anemia.

Cancer.

Malady one: a tendon in my right shoulder was knotted. If untreated I'd tear my rotator cuff. Back to physical therapy. Glenn and the staff remembered me from last fall.

("How's the chi running?")

At my initial session, Glenn massaged, kneaded, and stretched various ligaments and muscles. I left with an aching shoulder and a printed set of home exercises.

Malady two: anemia. My blood pressure was more depressed than Wall Street. Nakamura wasn't sure why but prescribed iron supplements.

Malady three cancer arrived in the wake of the dermatologist's biopsy report.

But not a coffin-stuffer like lymphoma. According to dermatologist Doctor Reznor, a young man two years into his practice, my nose was riddled with basal squamous. Basal squamous sounded like a Davos billionaire. But the cancer advanced. Metastasizing was a possibility, so an operation was scheduled.

Seven days later in early April, I lay on an examination bed, undergoing painful outpatient surgery. All manner of nerves crisscross the nose. That's why guys punch each other there. Even with a local anesthetic, it felt like a sharp blade stabbing my snout each time Reznor dug out more cancerous cells.

"Take that hook out," he'd say to his nurse, along with "blot."

Two passes were required for Reznor to carve out all the bad tissue. A skin graft was necessary to cover the nose wound. Reznor removed flesh from behind my ear. The basal squamous had been poised to spread into the nose cartilage. Then I might've died or spent the rest of my life as Beakless Bill. As it was, I went home with a huge nose bandage. Blood drained into my mouth. Everything I ate tasted like entrees at a vampire buffet.

Of course, now I had a 40 percent chance of reacquiring skin cancer. As my nose healed, I drifted into depression. It'd taken me a year to walk three miles. I still hadn't run since the knee surgery.

Point to Doctors Ang and Minu.

Even if running old school was out, I could barely walk the chi way. I was closing in on 60. And right that moment, I needed to make money. My professional career was in hospice. My short stories were finally selling, but they paid little. Joy couldn't land steady editing work.

I continued walking three times a week, pondering methods to stop the financial drain.

As for Malady one, physical therapy eventually restored a fair range of motion to my right shoulder. Nevertheless, sharp twinges reoccurred. Glenn suggested I continue with my shoulder homework.

Meanwhile, the skin graft on my nose turned blacker than a dog's snout. I looked like I'd fallen asleep on a propane torch. And the horrid thing itched.

After another blood test in May, I learned I was anemia free. And my right shoulder exhibited an almost normal range of motion. The Good News Hat Trick continued as Reznor removed the nose stitches. Admiring his work, he said another year would pass before the skin graft fully healed. I was cautioned to avoid long spells outdoors without sunblock.

Mid-May I visited a local high school track. No band director was around. Had Aaron ever squared away his blue circles? In life we must live with such mysteries. For instance, I still don't know what ignited Kim's cackle in the Phoenix Porta-Potty. But I was learning to embrace the unknown.

In the early evening, I walked as fast as I could for 1,600 meters, four laps, one mile.

11:28.

The knee was a bit sore, but not too bad. My mood brightened. Athletic possibilities suggested themselves. If you walk fast enough, eventually you'll run.

My agent lined up a few meetings. I met friendly, upbeat studio executives. (After all, they had jobs.) We parted on good terms. But no work.

And then it happened.

Walking fast one morning, I broke into a run, the first time since last year before my surgery. I made sure to switch my cadence from walking to running. A few days later, I ventured a mile again, adding a 1x2 run/walk for safety. The following week I tacked on a second running mile.

By late June, I'd added a third. This chi running was starting to take.

A thought arose that I should stop timing my miles. Chasing minutes was enjoyable: today faster than yesterday. But in chi running, speed is a byproduct of correct form. The further forward you lean, the faster you go. My form needed some work.

Next time out, I didn't record splits, running three miles without walk breaks: the first time I'd covered any distance minus walk breaks in two years. I'd felt relaxed, almost in the zone. No soreness. No spitlk. In a burst of excitement, I signed up for a 5k. Not Chapman, but a race I'd run before up in Santa Clarita.

Back in 2007, I'd finished the Independence Day Classic 5k in 25:04. Awarded a cotton tee-shirt—it was only a 5k—I continued my training, determined to break four hours that fall in the Windy City.

Suddenly, it was 2010 and I was lined up again for the Independence Day Classic. I hadn't run a 5k anywhere since that broiling '07 morning, and no racing period in two years. Now waiting for the start, I fidgeted, shaking my right leg, then my left. I'd never raced using the chi running method. I imagined people attacking me, trying to silence my metronome.

An air horn sounded and away dashed several hundred runners.

A cool morning with a marine layer; excellent running weather. A parade was set for later and the racecourse was decorated with American flags. Chi running focuses swarmed around my brain like moths attacking a porch light.

Running uphill, I shortened my stride, lengthened it downhill, and sped up on the flats. I leaned from my ankles like a ski jumper, only not so exaggerated. You'd have to pay attention to know I was tilted forward. In the last few hundred yards, I passed an older runner, then zipped around a teenage girl to finish in 29:37.

Amazing. Not even back running two months and I'd notched a sub-30-minute 5k. This chi running stuff was a miracle. No soreness or spitlk. My calves hurt, but I'd probably been landing too far forward on the balls of my feet. Anyway, I was back and bad.

Marinating in endorphins, I drove the wrong way home. But motoring away from the freeway didn't bother me. For all my recent gloom, I'd been right on the doorstep of a killer comeback. Eventually, I located the correct onramp and drove home, plump with positive feelings.

The following week Joy was hired to edit articles on a new website. For the first time in years, steady money flowed into the household. I'd sold another short story and picked up a small job writing jokes for a rookie comic. Plus, I'd lost weight, dropping back to 223 pounds.

I continued running three times a week. Every session featured me acting like an idiot. Enthusiasm overrode common sense. I pretended every run was the Santa Clarita 5k.

A part of me was yelling to ease up. Train don't race. But I ran as if I were back in junior high. One afternoon the coach had set up folding chairs in each corner of the gym. Our task was to run one mile on the outside of the chairs. This would be my first run over a measured distance. Unlike rope climbing or pull-ups where I lacked upper body strength, running seemed to have been waiting for me. While not the quickest, I ran all out, fast and hard, rounding the chairs, passing stronger boys who gasped and walked. I felt mighty that day.

The joy I'd experienced in the gym that day was back. No more running, huh? Quit, huh? Do something else, huh? Throttling down took more discipline than I possessed. My chi running form slipped. Heel striking crept back.

In mid-August, pain reared up in BOTH knees. Ice and rest followed.

A week passed and I joined some runners racing along the Arroyo Seco Channel. I hustled so as not to be last. Suddenly the Great Heel Pounder was back. Spitlk. For the rest of August and into September, I slowed way down, iced the left knee, and reinstituted run/walks.

Run, spitlk, rest, ice, run, spitlk.

Too little, too late.

Tendonitis flared up again in my right shoulder. Halloween arrived. After weeks of sporadic exercise, all the weight I'd lost had returned with interest.

Fearful of doing something else ill-considered, I skipped the Chapman 5k. About that time, Joy's job burned through their funding and stopped paying. She responded by not working. Thanksgiving found our finances once more drawn tight. Gym membership went on hold, and I canceled Netflix. Our microwave died. My debt-heavy credit card provided a new one.

Nothing stings like a self-inflicted defeat. After July 4th, I let my worst instincts dominate. Months of incremental gain were tossed away for a few fun weeks.

On Veterans Day, my friend Karen called from Florida. She phoned every November 11th. It was our yearly catch-up call. In the '70s, Karen and I had worked together at the post office back in Skokie, Illinois. For the last several years, her health had been terrible, her body racked by a bouquet of exotic debilitating illnesses. But no one handled misfortune better. Karen's good cheer and upbeat spirit were infectious. I felt less downbeat about my running woes.

Around Christmas, I planned my 2011 schedule.

Measured progress worked. I'd start again and build on that.

For the new year, I scheduled gradual increases in monthly and weekly mileage, cadence bpm, run/walk ratios, and mileage long runs. I penciled in four 5ks: one in May attached to the Pasadena Marathon, a second again up in Santa Clarita for July 4th, a September race in Santa Monica, and a Thanksgiving turkey trot out in Calabasas. These 5ks would give me mini goals to shoot for and help focus my training.

Lots of elements in my Project Run-Again schedule, but this time I'd move slow and steady.

Stick to the plan.

Chapter Four

2011

B est Picture: *The King's Speech*
Super Bowl Champ: Green Bay Packers
Billboard Top Song: "Rolling in the Deep" by Adele
U.S. President: Barack H. Obama
Top Web Browser: Internet Explorer

> "Knowledge rests not upon truth alone, but upon error also."

— Carl Jung

Every major kitchen appliance was terminal.

Our refrigerator motor periodically erupted into humming and rattling like a robot singing the blues. The washing machine throbbed as if about to shake itself across the kitchen and out the front door to a better funded house.

We cashed in most of the money market funds. Longingly, I eyed my 401k. To siphon off funds without a nasty tax bite, one needed to be aged 59 and a half. For once, I was too young for something.

In January, I undertook two steps to improve our finances.

But first, Project Run-Again.

As the year commenced, I plodded three miles using a 1x2 run/walk. Knowing that timing runs led to speedy temptations, I stopped wearing my Ironman sports watch. Each week the Run-Again plan contained much to remember: cadence, run/walk ratio, total mileage, long run. I also felt compelled to add a goal weight. Over last fall and Christmas, my weight had inched back into the 230s. I felt like an aging dumpling.

While using barbells, I felt a sharp pain in my right shoulder. Back to Nakamura who punted me once more to the orthopedist. More x-rays, examinations, prodding, and kneading by the always-tardy Doctor Weddell. ("Sorry I'm late. Does this hurt?") Weddell discovered a bone spur sawing its way through a tendon. I could wait until it succeeded or undergo another arthroscopic surgery.

Health issues were becoming a grim perennial. Exasperated with the operation *du jour*, I agreed to shoulder surgery but pushed it back to May. At least I could follow Project Run-Again up to Pasadena. A good 5k finish time would lighten the post-op blahs. I looked forward to seeing supportive Glenn once more at physical therapy.

Since I knew where most of the equipment was, I considered asking him for a part-time job.

Back to those financial steps: number one involved recommitting to TV animation. I met my agent Julie for breakfast. Over my fourth cup of coffee, Julie mentioned the painfully obvious: animation writers in their late 50s aren't very marketable. But you can't sell a show if you don't try. I needed to brainstorm ten ideas for an animated series. A sentence or two apiece. From those, we'd choose a couple to be fleshed out and pitched around to the studios. If nothing else, I'd meet the latest crop of gatekeepers. These were executives who knew executives who did the hiring.

Financial step number two involved writing marketing copy. I saw something on the Web defining marketing copy as "written information that aims to inform, persuade, or entertain an audience." Sure. Okay. Fiction writer, copywriter, same thing, yes? But certain gross differences existed.

In fiction writing, you tease the readers, respecting their familiarity with genres, tropes, and the works of better authors than yourself. Attract their eyes onto the next sentence, paragraph, page, scene, all the way to The End.

In copywriting, you crack the reader over the skull with a club and keep swinging. Repeat a few simple points, then drive them home like tent stakes. It's the difference between badminton on a lawn and brawling on a dock with razors. Plus, my young marketing bosses weren't keen on training. They came from the sink or swim school of writing. In you go, hope it works out. That's how they'd learned. That's how they taught me.

Copywriting money was okay. But the sheer amount of material required per job—long letters, short emails, landing pages, upsells, videos—all crammed with an unfamiliar product and delivered under killer deadlines—had me longing for a TV animation script with knot-headed executive notes. Each project felt like sprinting in my socks on wet plexiglass.

Across the Pacific, tsunamis crashed into Fukushima. In the City of Angels I soldiered on, writing copy, plus ideas for animated TV shows. Oh, and training for my 5k. This would be a pilot fish race, attached to the Pasadena Marathon. Thrice a week I continued shuffling along, rarely reaching three miles.

My friend Bernadette was also training for Pasadena in May. She planned on doing the marathon with her teenage daughter. The daughter was an athlete but not a distance runner. Bernadette tried explaining the necessity of long runs. In addition to allowing runners to practice vital tasks such as hydrating and refueling, long runs build confidence and patience. The body grows accustomed to the stress of lifting both feet up and down for hours. But the daughter wasn't all that into long runs. After all, she'd played high school soccer. ("Really, Mom, we used to run the whole game.") She knew about marathons the way I'd known about copywriting.

In April, I increased my run/walk ratio to two minutes running and one walking. A week later, I bumped it up to 3x1. Four miles now constituted my long run. Angry at another surgery, I was determined to finish strong at Pasadena. Frustrated, I pushed myself. My chi running form grew sloppy.

Agent Julie selected three of my ideas. She felt they met that year's mercurial industry criteria. Like dress codes among teenage girls, studio themes changed often. One year a new series should be "empowering," the next year "wish fulfilling" or "promotes cattle insemination." In any event, you wanted that year's element in your story pitches. While Julie lined up May meetings with Cartoon Network's Adult Swim, Disney XD, the Disney Channel, and Nickelodeon, I fleshed out the three ideas.

Each idea was expanded into five or six pages containing a series synopsis, characters, setting, and sample episodes. You wanted to provide only enough material to tease the executive palate. Hopefully, that would lead to a studio paying you to write a sample script and a show bible. Until that point, you were working on your own time. But the potential payoff was hefty.

Another May, another stinking medical procedure. Shoulder surgery was scheduled for two weeks after the Pasadena 5k. Again, a good chunk of the year would be lost to recovery and physical therapy. Three years of stop-and-go training were grinding my motivation to a fine silt. Financial pressures, coupled with copywriting and pitch deadlines, were squeezing me like a rock python. The pressure appeared in my running. I pushed harder than necessary.

Hello, spitlk.

I stopped running. Rest. Ice. Resume walking at a lower intensity. Pasadena was a week away. Disgusted with running, I elected to walk the 5k. I'd be happy just finishing. How did the running I once loved become something I wanted to strangle with a wire? Many relationships tragically ended on that question.

Pitching was underway. I memorized the high points of each of my series ideas, including the studio's current element. I never brought out the little pitch booklet until the end. I wanted the execs listening. More importantly, I wanted them to ask questions. Things seemed to go well with the first two pitches.

On a cool, drizzly Sunday morning, I loped across the finish line at 41:18. That's a 13:17 pace which placed me exactly in the middle of my age group. On the final mile, I beat out a 79-year-old man and an eight-year-old girl and challenged a woman pushing a stroller, but she dropped me in the home stretch. To my astonishment, the event handed out finisher medals. For a 5k! That's like being rewarded for humming. In celebration of completing my first race in almost a year, I accepted the lousy medal.

I wouldn't accept any more for a long time.

Bernadette and her very weary daughter became marathoners that day. Meanwhile, I bumped into Coach

Kate. That morning, Kate had run the half-marathon, coming in third among women, crossing the timing mat at 1:29:03. She was kicking back, watching her husband Jimmy wrangle a group of novice runners through their first 5k.

Last summer, while I ran Santa Clarita, Kate's husband Jimmy had been preparing to tackle the Badwater Ultramarathon. Runners begin in Death Valley, then cross three mountain ranges in temperatures that can top 120 degrees. The race ends 135 miles away at the trailhead to Mt. Whitney. On the home stretch, Jimmy stood off challenges from two other runners to finish 15th overall. Impressive athleticism, true, but he lacked my broad insight into the medical profession.

The next two weeks were a blur of marketing deadlines, a few more animation pitch meetings, and unmotivated stationary cycling. Finally, the new operation arrived. It was surgery in the morning, and home again in the afternoon. With a massive sling on my right arm and a belly full of cool drugs, I stared at the TV.

Floating in a post-op haze, here's what I watched that day from my comfy chair.

I Shouldn't Be Alive
A biography of John Candy
Two-hour special on snipers
Scared Straight!
Two hours of *Storage Wars*

Dog the Bounty Hunter was on deck, but I slumbered from my medication, sitting upright per doctor's orders.

A few days later, aching shoulder and all, I headed to my next pitch. Joy drove me over to the Cartoon Network. The young executive was affable, laughing after I said the sling on my arm justified handicapped parking. After listening to my idea about a Viking detective named Jack Odin, he expressed both interest and a noncommittal attitude—a real pro.

By months end, I'd completed Pitch Fest '11. Three ideas had been pitched to five studios. Two of those ideas generated a trio of "maybes." That meant executives would hash those ideas over with colleagues before a formal rejection was issued to my agent.

Several of my short stories were accepted into anthologies. Those placements provided a pleasing contrast to the barren conclusion of Pitch Fest '11. As for exercise, by July, the doctors had greenlit me for stationary cycling and easy walking.

Money rolled in from marketing, but the copywriting gigs were erratic. As said, each assignment arrived suddenly, and every job was a rush job with a hard deadline.

Joy worked for a time with a graphic designer on another website project. This time the money spigot never turned on, though emails saying "next week for sure" were plentiful. Joy withdrew her services.

After selling our home in '08, we'd kept a storage unit filled with boxes of stuff. To save money, I canceled the unit and brought the stuff home. Now we lived in a box maze.

In September, Occupy Wall Street brought countless hours of drumming and piles of trash to the neighbors of Zuccotti Park. After a series of spitlks, I quit walking, then stopped exercising altogether. Instead, I focused on my strong points of eating and depression. There was clearly something flawed with this chi running/walking. It sucked. What was the point of practicing if the lousy knee always hurt? From the depths of my lounge chair, I determined not to attempt any more runs—chi or otherwise—until I'd shed 40 pounds. (At the time I weighed 251.)

Veterans Day rolled around and, once again, my friend Karen left a phone message. We hadn't seen each other since her 1994 wedding. A few days before the ceremony, Karen, her sister, and I had tromped out into the Everglades orchid-hunting. I knew from her blog that health issues had been rockier than usual. Despite assistance from her husband, Karen couldn't move far without a special motorized chair. And yet she'd recently managed a solo trip to Home Depot, picked up a dandelion weeder, and put in a little time in her garden. Back in August, Karen had blogged that "happiness is good and right and belongs to us, that we can, and should, understand it and seek it out."

Why did I have so much trouble choosing happiness? Copywriting had staunched the year's financial hemorrhage. Those vexing upsells and email blasts had staved off worse fates. We'd even restarted Netflix and the gym membership. Those were blessings worth counting.

December arrived, and I forced myself back to short walks and stationary cycling. But no union animation work meant we'd burned through our health care as well as COBRA. (Consolidated Omnibus Budget Reconciliation Act, a federal law allowing you to keep your health care for eighteen months provided you paid out-of-pocket. Very expensive.) Having since closed my Subchapter S corporation, Joy and I were in medical freefall.

"Whatever you do," I said, "don't get sick."

"Look who's talking?"

2012 was rumored to be the end of the world.

Or the end of the world for Mayans.

We'd find out soon enough.

Chapter Five

2012

Best Picture: *The Artist*
Super Bowl Champ: New York Giants
Billboard Top Song: "Somebody That I Used to Know"
by Gotye
U.S. President: Barack H. Obama
Top Web Browser: Internet Explorer/Chrome

> "It is said that the night brings counsel, but it is
> not said that the counsel is necessarily good."

— Jules Verne

Like leaves in a Santa Ana, my old teammates had float-
ed off.

Coaches, captains, and participants I'd known had
moved on to ultramarathons or Ironman triathlons, mar-

riage, kids, and careers. Only a handful remained. And while many of the San Gabriel Valley Marathon crew were on social media, I was wary of the media's time-sapping abilities. Nothing could replace the solidarity of training and racing. The circle of people I talked about running with drew tighter than my old slacks. Ernesto was one of the few.

We'd both joined the team in the fall of 2005. Along with Boston CJ, we'd trained together, run our rookie marathon in Honolulu, then trained and raced on subsequent teams. Since 2007, Ernesto and I had been meeting for Saturday breakfast at a Pasadena coffee shop.

Husky, built like the high-school defensive tackle he'd once been, Ernesto's last marathon had been Los Angeles 2010. Since then, he'd been sidelined with Achilles Tendon issues. At breakfast, we'd still talk teammates and races, but we'd become distance running voyeurs. As our active participation waned, movies, USC football, and internet memes dominated most Saturday morning conversations. Still, if I said I really missed marathons, Ernesto would know exactly what I meant.

At first, I never understood the marathon.

It was a long exhausting run I wanted to finish; an accomplishment to brag about. You show up in shorts and run. Having approached a marathon once, I'd parked it in the back of my mind for decades. Periodically, the marathon would awaken to ask, "Now?" only to be returned to hibernation.

Then came Team in Training.

Having completed five marathons, I realized that when runners celebrate crossing the finish line, it's not just for 26.2. They're also acclaiming a successful commitment to months of training with its aches and injuries, mishaps, physical and mental challenges. To say the marathon was just running was like saying a house was only the exterior.

But finishing a marathon now seemed as impossible as vacationing in the Orion Nebula. I couldn't even cover three miles consistently. When my *Runners World* subscription lapsed, I didn't renew. Bundling up the old issues, I passed them on to Ernesto.

I worked out on the treadmill and stationary bike. Pool running and swimming were also on the training schedule, along with a few walks. But as another presidential election year commenced, my days were absorbed in marketing. A landslide of copywriting swept across my desk. Perhaps there was a rush to sell things before the world ended in December. (As mentioned, the Maya Doomsday Calendar and theories of an environmental catastrophe were red hot. They even made a movie about it.)

Life fell into a routine of finishing a copywriting project, invoicing, and starting another.

Passive Income Websites!
Earn Like You've Always Dreamed!
No Experience Needed for Super App!
Money Pouring in While You Sleep!

Webinars were in high demand. I'd write all the dialogue, including questions from the "callers." And, of course, there were email swipes by the hundreds. I found them to be the typing equivalent of chloroform.

In February, I attempted a run.

After walking a mile, I ran a second mile using a 1x 2 run/walk. No spitlk. I was so pleased that I did it again two days later, only faster. No knee pains. My mind whirled with visions of increasing mileage and speed.

But that Friday, my knee hurt. Not spitlk, but a dull ache such as I'd experienced last year. Once again, rest, ice, plan. What could I do differently?

I decided to measure progress by time instead of distance. Continuing into March, I walked 30 minutes twice a week. Along with cross-training, that seemed about all the time my beleaguered left knee could handle. In April, I ventured a third walk each week. No spitlk.

At the same time, my animation writing career took a surprising turn: it improved.

An old Warner Bros. colleague was producing a show for Nickelodeon. (This producer was a networking dynamo.) In his Burbank office, this producer said, "Our staff writers are burned out. Our A-list freelancers are burned out. We need you to come up with new ideas."

After me, the next step was advertising for writers on Craigslist.

Still, I was grateful for a shot. A union job meant union benefits. Joy and I would be covered once more by the

Motion Picture Industry Health Plan. In between copy-writing, I churned out story ideas regarding the adventures of a pudgy panda bear who practices kung fu.

Unexpectedly, another Warner Bros. alum called. He'd been developing an animated series for Disney. The series had been greenlit. I was in line for a staff position. I hadn't worked a staff job in seven years. The thought of a steady paycheck left me weak and giddy. Joy and I could buy new clothes, take a vacation, or purchase quieter appliances. Before I could begin on staff, I would be required to have two scripts approved. At that moment, I was a writing machine. Two scripts comin' up!

For the next few frenzied weeks, I worked on the marketing copy, the Nick script, and the first of the Disney scripts. The Nickelodeon producer approved an idea, so away I went to outline. For Disney, I turned in several story ideas and waited.

My right shoulder continued healing from surgery. After a year, I could almost reach the center of my back. Unfortunately, skin cancer issues continued.

Doctor Reznor flagged a spot on my lower left leg as precancerous. That meant he'd spotted an abnormal-looking section of skin that could precede the formation of cancer. Curettage and electrodesiccation were indicated.

Known as a scrape and burn, the procedure involves the dermatologist using a spoon-shaped instrument called a curette to scrape the affected skin surface. After carving out the precancerous tissues, Reznor cauterized the region. The scrape and burn left an ugly divot in my lower left calf. And the wound stunk. My stinky divot healed at a glacial pace. No swimming for several weeks.

Copywriting remained at high boil with more webinars, phone apps, and other new products. Nickelodeon approved my outline, and I went to script. Disney approved an idea, and I went to outline. During all this, I wrote and submitted a short crime story on the price of hipness. A dark story anthology grabbed it up. I wish all my fiction landed so fast.

Just before the summer Olympics, I walked around the Rose Bowl. I covered three miles in 46:07. The following week, I walked two miles, then ran one. I felt good and spitlk-free. For the next five weeks I'd walk twice a week, then run three miles every Friday, using a 1x2 run/walk.

In the men's Olympic marathon in London, American marathon record holder Ryan Hall dropped out at mile 11 with hamstring issues. Hall's teammate, Meb Keflezighi, an old man of 37, was coming off an injury. Ready to quit at mile 13, he changed his thinking mid-race to focus on the positives. With 5k remaining, Keflezighi surged, picking off two runners and finishing fourth.

That brought something to mind. I'd integrated positive thinking into my training for Phoenix. Couldn't I up my mental game? Just then, having lots of paying work put me in a positive mood. I let the mental-game upgrade drop.

August saw my Nick script approved. In addition, the studio bought a few additional story springboards. At Disney, my outline had been approved. I'd gone to script one.

Around that time, my friend Karen passed away. Her husband Walter had died of brain cancer three months earlier. A brutal shot, but if anyone could survive such a crippling blow, I believed it was Karen. I was wrong. Officially, she succumbed to infection, but her nephew felt Walter's departure left a deep hole Karen had no wish to fill.

Karen's loss rocked me like a chest punch. Depression and self-pity returned like unwanted relatives. Negative thoughts unrolled their sleeping bags and took up residence. What was the point of running? *My left knee would always be tender. I couldn't master chi running. Rest, ice, start again trapped me in a hellish loop.* I finally said aloud what I'd been feeling for some time: I quit.

I quit marathons or the hope of attempting another marathon. It was now officially a memory, something I did "back then," medals on a wall.

For good measure, I quit running. Thanks for the fun times. Don't bother to call. I'd stay in shape with the elliptical machine, stationary biking, and the occasional walk.

By October, the marketing jobs vanished. A week would pass, and I'd expect to hear from this or that marketer—they shared everything, including me. But the spigot had closed. Meanwhile, script one had been approved by Disney.

November 11 arrived. The phone remained silent. I had no interest in exercise. My weight returned to the mid-250s. I wore sweatpants everywhere like an Italian mobster.

In late December, life continued without world-cracking environmental doom. The dark stories anthology published my short crime tale. To paraphrase pulp author Robert E. Howard: In a cosmos engulfed by stygian blackness, here shone a small glittering light. (Howard used "stygian" the way Lovecraft used "eldritch." Find an obscure word and beat it into the ground.)

For the first time in five years, I'd made decent money. Nevertheless, getting up in the morning was a chore. Every task, no matter how minor, seemed to require excessive amounts of energy. Days were interrupting my sleep.

I'd had better years.

Chapter Six

2013

B est Picture: *Argo*
Super Bowl Champ: Baltimore Ravens
Billboard Hot 100 Top Single: "Thrift Shop" by Macklemore and Ryan Lewis
U.S. President: Barack H. Obama (Second Term)
Top Web Browser: Google Chrome

> "It must be borne in mind that the tragedy of life doesn't lie in not reaching your goal. The tragedy lies in having no goals to reach."

— Benjamin E. Mays

Author Hal Higdon first completed the Boston Marathon in 1959.

He was one of 198 runners. (Almost 30k participated in 2021.) Higdon wrote for *Runner's World* and helped popularize the sport. His book, *On the Run from Dogs and People*, speaks "of an era [unknown] to today's runners—when runners were so rare along our byways that people did taunt us . . . and dogs took time to assault us . . . "

After being discharged from the Marines in the mid-70s, I returned home to Skokie, a northern Chicago suburb. Despite a smoking habit and a fondness for drink, I'd run around parks, Forest Preserve paths, and city blocks. Dogs might pursue, but no one taunted me. Of course, 20 years later, people would yell, "Run, Forrest, run," but time and good taste silenced them.

While attending Oakton Junior College, I landed a job with the post office. I worked on the loading dock pushing around bulk mail containers and forklifting wooden pallets of glossy magazines into trucks. Every afternoon I'd zip around town in an AMC truck, emptying the corner mailboxes. This was called "picking up the drops." Several of us drove separate routes. Rain or shine, we'd open the boxes and stuff letters into canvas sacks. In winter, we'd need to kick the mailbox keyholes to loosen the ice. Should snowplows bury the boxes, we'd claw through the powder like wolverines to retrieve the mail. On the coldest days, Karen, myself, and the other drivers would emerge from our trucks with rime-coated mufflers, looking like German prisoners at Stalingrad.

Quitting cigarettes drew me to distance running.

At first, I'd participate in 5ks held along the bike trails near Northwestern University. To find a race, I'd check the back of the *Chicago Tribune* sports section. Somewhere in a sea of microscopic print, there'd be an event listed for the upcoming weekend. Then off to Evanston for a Sunday morning dash with other runners. Each race attracted a field that might fill a city bus. But that was no slur on the popularity of running. It was hot and growing hotter.

At the recent '76 Olympics, defending champ Frank Shorter had won marathon silver while teammate Don Kardong missed bronze by three seconds. Running fever spread across America. As Shorter wrote years later in *Runners Magazine*, "My previously arcane discipline, the marathon, had sprouted into a trend, a movement, a sport, and a pastime . . . Across the nation, thousands of ordinary citizens now trained virtually as hard as I did. Both from a spectator and participant perspective, the marathon was no longer a virgin, unexplored continent."

In 1977, the Director of Cardiac Rehabilitation at a local hospital organized the Ravenswood Bank Lakefront 10-Mile Run. Expecting a few hundred souls for the May event, good doctor Noel Nequin discovered his creation had attracted over a thousand. I found the race in the back of the Tribune. Sending in a few bucks, the organizers mailed me a bib with my race number and a cotton T-shirt. I was in.

Being young, I never pondered my running ignorance. My formal training had been thin. In high school, I'd joined the track team. To be precise, I'd only trained with the track team. In January, with snow drifts piled high and wind gusts slicing your face like paper cuts, we'd run the icy streets around the school. On the coldest days, we'd run the bleachers in the gym in a ruthless cycle, clambering up and down, thighs burning, breath hot and raw. But I was very involved with my first sweetheart back then—beer. Also, my girlfriend and I weren't getting along. Eventually, I quit track to party. I already knew how to run the streets.

Back to the Lakefront 10. I calculated that if the race were ten miles, then I'd train by running eleven or twelve or thirteen. Not surprisingly, 11-12-13 miles equaled the distance of the drop routes from the post office and back. I knew them all by heart. And since my apartment was a few blocks from the office, I needed only to open the front door and go.

That March, I began training for the Lakefront 10-Mile Run. Three mornings a week, I'd slug down a protein drink and then run around melting snow drifts from one mailbox to another. In April, the weather warmed, and humidity turned the air sodden. I thought hydration applied to crops not running. Consuming water while exercising seemed a moral failure. In boot camp, you'd run with a full canteen. At the run's end, the water better be untouched. I never carried water.

How I dodged heat exhaustion is a mystery. I relied on water fountains in parks and the faucet in gas station washrooms. And no Ironman sports watches. While I later carried a stopwatch, I trained for the Lakefront 10 until I ran out of mailboxes.

On a sunny May morning, my girlfriend and I drove into the city to Belmont Harbor. I'd never seen so many runners in one place not wearing green uniforms. Pacing was another alien concept. When the race started, I ran as fast as I could. Along a route that followed more of Chicago's ubiquitous bike paths, I spied water stations. How charming! I'd grab a cup and go.

So many runners! I wasted considerable energy weaving in and out of the pack. There were no strollers, dogs, or people dressed like Marvel superheroes on the course. Only runners. An out-and back-affair, I reached the turn-around point, doubled back, and eventually zipped across the finish line. No bagels, orange slices, space blankets, bananas, bottled water, photographers, tacos, waffles, beer, or medals awaited me. You were done. Now go home. Don't make a big deal about it.

My girlfriend snapped a photo, and we left to catch some movie called *Star Wars*. Days later, my big toenails fell off. Swelling feet butting against the toe box of my shoes caused this interesting microtrauma.

A few weeks after the race, I received an envelope in the mail. Inside was a mimeographed list of Lakefront 10 finishing times. I'd clocked 72 minutes, 7:12 a mile. Was that bad or good? I didn't know any other runners to ask. But I knew I wanted another distance challenge.

I started reading *Runner's World*. I learned about the Boston Marathon. *What a cool sounding race.* In those pages, I first encountered Bill Rodgers, who'd shortly notch three Boston victories in a row.

Locally, Doctor Noel Nequin continued planning. Now he'd organized a marathon right there in Chicago. In fact, the inaugural event was scheduled for that September.

An old proverb goes that every January memberships increase for gyms and AA. As 2013 began, I noted that my local gym featured rows of treadmills, stationary cycles, Stairmasters, and a few ellipticals, many lacking Out-of-Order signs. I'd warm up by driving around looking for a parking spot, then walking several blocks to the gym. First the rowing machine, some crunches, then the stair master, finishing up with stationary cycling or the elliptical. For the sake of nostalgia, I incorporated treadmill workouts. Low speed, clump along; listen to my iPod. Not many calories burned, but no spitlk.

Depression kept stopping by to borrow a cup of well-being. Of course, depression brought its dear friend, Weight Gain. My exercise regimen was sporadic. Fortunately, my sweatpants ensemble rose to meet the challenge.

In February, I commenced a 12-week program running on the treadmill. My goal was to drop 30 pounds—ever the optimist. At least, there shouldn't be any spitlk.

Financial concerns required my attention. While marketing work returned, it was a shadow of 2012. As to last year's Disney job, I was never able to get a second story idea approved. That meant our credit cards put on additional pounds, often carrying the burden for groceries.

Joy was still smarting from another website bust. Brought in as editor-in-chief, she'd been given carte blanche to write articles, edit copy, sell ads, and boost clicks. However, her juvenile partners undermined that authority by whimsically changing the banner artwork or inadvertently erasing the page view metrics. Joy finally left the team, leaving the website to crumble without adult guidance.

Giant Amazon had entered the animation realm and was looking for properties. Agent Julie set up a meeting. I dusted off a few TV animation ideas from the 2011 Pitch Fest. Then I added a couple of new ones. I rehearsed their presentation, thought positive, and went in energetic. The Amazon executive was young and friendly. She was also uninterested in my ideas.

Come April, news broke of the Boston Marathon bombing. Three died, including an eight-year-old boy, plus over 260 were injured. A seven-year-old girl had her leg blown off. I was furious. Of the two radical Islamic bombers, one was later shot by cops and fell dying in the street.

His fleeing brother ran him over in a car. Wounded and captured, the surviving sibling now sits in prison. He might be executed. Until then, he's parked in a supermax, slowly aging, year after year, playing checkers with the Unabomber.

Like a bad ex-girlfriend, running lingered in my mind.

Lounging around the sensory cortex in a slinky negligee, running would whisper, coo, entice, promising sizzling days ahead if I'd only return. Oh, sultry tart running; oh, painted harlot.

Ten months after quitting forever, I ran.

Steady treadmill work through May and June failed to induce spitlk or soreness. So, I decided to venture 40 minutes of movement. During said time, I would incorporate run/walks at 1x2. Could I even handle such minimal exercise?

I could and did.

Throughout July, I managed four such sessions without soreness or spitlk. Exercise, in general, suffered as I typed away, trying to finish an e-book for Amazon Kindle.

In August, I managed five run/walk sessions.

In September, seven sessions.

Feeling encouraged, I upped the run/walk ratio to 2x2. In October, I ventured four minutes running for every minute walked.

A month later, I ran 2.5 miles. No run/walk, cadence, or splits. It was my first sustained effort in two years.

Like running the drop routes, I recorded no times. Most importantly, there was no soreness or spitlk.

Run/walks increased to 6x1 in December. Session times grew to 55 minutes. Once again, a long period away from running was followed by seeming improvement. But I questioned whether it would be sustainable.

The year finished on a high note. My mother-in-law took pity on Joy and me. She bought us several quieter appliances. The silence in our kitchen was deafening.

Before Christmas, I published my first e-book. Culled from a series of blog posts, I'd fashioned them into an essay. Having set lofty publishing goals in January, I was nowhere near the mark. But at least I finished one e-book.

Santa brought me my very own stationary bike. I set about crafting a poor man's Peloton. First, I'd position the bike in front of my laptop. Then log onto YouTube. Then click on the Global Cycling Network. Then peddle away with encouragement from GCN's British instructors.

Compared to last year, my overall health seemed better. My weight was down a bit. The right shoulder had healed, and the skin cancer stayed manageable. I'd emerged from a long spell of depression. I'd turned a corner. Of course, if your life consists of walking in squares, you're always turning a corner.

Chapter Seven

2014

Best Picture: *12 Years a Slave*
Super Bowl Champ: Seattle Seahawks
Billboard Hot 100 Top Single: "The Monster" by Eminem
U.S. President: Barack H. Obama
Top Web Browser: Google Chrome

> "I don't feel old. I don't feel anything till noon.
> That's when it's time for my nap."

> — Bob Hope

Paying jobs ended their boycott.

Copywriting swelled with its many emails and upsells. I also completed a second e-book and hawked it around the web. My online sales approach was as subtle as my copywriting, "Hey, buy this book, okay? Yeah, you. This book, right here. Buy it."

Time management in the digital age was becoming an issue. My suspicion of social media as a time suck was confirmed. I blogged then: "As an independent author, I need to establish my presence online. But I find the balance hard to maintain. I should be focusing on the final rewrites to my next e-book. . . Instead, I've spent the past ninety minutes "liking" the Facebook and Amazon author pages of other writers, screwing around with Twitter and Goodreads and wondering when I'll get over to Google+. My online presence is not large, but all the likes and comments add up. A hundred small leaks will cause a boat to founder as surely as a great hole."

In addition, January and February brought a pair of small jobs for two new animated series at DreamWorks and Warner Bros. That much industry work hadn't hit my desk since 2012. And while minor development pay was minuscule, the union hours might eventually add up toward health care.

I did a few run/walk sessions. But other than the occasional stationary bike ride, physical fitness wasn't a priority. But even the little stationary cycling I did left my knee sore. Not spitlk, but a dull ache. Had five years of spasmodic exercise eroded the fibrocartilage?

Ang and Minu looked like prophets. They'd probably send me a photo of them laughing in their lab coats with the inscription, "Told You So." I figured I'd need another MRI.

In March, Joy and I took the closest thing to a vacation we'd had in years. We drove out to the desert for a spot of Indian gaming. Past Banning, in a wide valley between the peaks of San Gorgonio and San Jacinto, sits a hotel casino. This towering structure rose from a sea of factory outlets like a garish pagan monument of old. I hadn't been inside a casino in a while and didn't know the slot machines issued script. No more merry jangle of coins striking metal—just electronic boobs and beeps announcing the siphoning of money.

Toward the end of April, after a ten-year battle with liver cancer, my first cousin Mary Ann died. We'd been close since childhood. There wasn't a birthday, Christmas, or St. Patrick's Day that didn't see a card from Mary Ann. I'd stayed with her back when I ran the Chicago Marathon. In the end, Mary Ann grew weary of the chemo battering. Quitting treatment, she stayed at home on Foster Avenue and waited for the Reaper.

After a dreary flight back to the Windy City, I stayed at a hotel in the Village of Skokie near the funeral home. My father had moved our family to Skokie from Chicago in 1960 to work as an administrator in a new post office. My Irish nurse mother took work at Teletype Corporation, a huge plant known best for manufacturing electromechanical printers. Alas, Skokie, like America, was no longer into making things. Where Teletype, and its vast employee parking lots, once stood was now a great shopping mall. This mall was similar in design to another large shopping mall around my hotel.

Of course, I drove by the post office. A one-story brick building with opaque green windows, a flagpole, and a recruiting poster out front, that institution had fed my family for decades. My father had retired from there. My brother had worked as a mail carrier. Another first cousin, Mary Ann's brother, threw mail as a clerk. Another distant cousin also carried mail. I saw the concrete loading dock and the wells where the trucks backed in. Memories swirled around that building like mist coiled on an ancient lake.

Returning to LA, I noticed my sweatpants felt snug. A step on the scale revealed that I now weighed a portly 265 pounds. There was a crying need for action. I embarked on my first diet. Sitting in front of a computer screen all day minus snacks would prove to be a serious challenge.

A year after the bombing, an old man by the name of Meb Keflezighi won the Boston Marathon. He was the first American to win in 31 years. Back in the day, Americans often won the big marathons like Boston and New York City. But for whatever reason, U.S. distance running declined in the mid-80s, continuing a downward slide through the '90s as East Africans rose to dominate. At the 2004 Olympics, Meb's marathon silver marked the first time an American male had medaled since Frank Shorter back in my 5k days. (Deena Kastor took the women's bronze.) It seemed U.S. distance running was on a re-bound.

With the arrival of June, the paying jobs dried up. No more animation or marketing and nothing on the horizon. In anticipation of impending lean times, we canceled Netflix and the gym. I stopped buying books on Amazon and patronized the library. I worked on a collection of dark urban short stories, marketing my e-books, and resenting the stinking diet.

Summertime also kicked off another Carousel of Medical Fun. Thanks to the Nickelodeon script, I'd been back on Motion Picture Health Insurance since September 2012. Unfortunately, my union jobs earlier that year didn't provide enough hours for renewal. Having almost burned through COBRA, we'd be without health insurance come September 30th.

Joy and I had ridden the Carousel before. We each listed our health needs. I soon had appointments with my dentist, optometrist, chiropractor, dermatologist Reznor, Nakamura for a physical, gastroenterologist for a colonoscopy, and Weddell the orthopedist. I still wanted that MRI.

At Weddell's office, his incredibly chipper nurse would deposit you in an examination room. Sitting alone, glancing at bone charts, so much time would pass that it felt like a monastic retreat. On the day of my appointment, I brought a well-stocked Kindle device, plus old x-rays and images from my previous MRI. In addition, RN Nurse Karla had supplied me with a key phrase.

Sixty-three minutes after my scheduled appointment time, Dr. Weddle entered the examination room. "Sorry for being late. Your left knee is sore?"

"It's affecting my Quality of Life."

He paused. The pause continued. For a moment, I thought Weddle was paralyzed. Then he said, "What is it exactly you want to do?"

(Run a stinking marathon.)

"Oh, you know, walk a bit, ride a stationary bike. Quality of life stuff."

Did the key phrase do the trick? Probably not. In any case, I was soon back inside the giant egg roll.

A week later, I learned I had a "subtle blunting/fraying of the inner free edge of the mid-zone of the lateral meniscus." Also, "the medial meniscus remains intact." Deciphering, Weddle explained that the MRI showed no deterioration of the fibrocartilage. The knee appeared fine. What a relief.

Weddle offered me physical therapy. By mid-July, I was back chatting with triathlete therapist Glenn. Always of good cheer, he suggested I take my 2009 leg exercises and implement them several times a week. I liked Glenn. He always believed I could run again. It was encouraging. Hardly anyone I knew talked about running. Twice a week, Glenn's team worked on shoring up my left hip and glutes.

At the same time, a blood test from my physical showed a rise in PSA levels. PSA stood for prostate-specific antigen. It was a protein produced by cells in the prostate gland. Nakamura referred me to a urologist. Why not? I was seeing everyone else in a white coat.

Agent Julie reported all was quiet on the animation front. A few small marketing jobs couldn't stop the money lasso from tightening. From my 401k, I withdrew a large chunk. Joy landed copyediting gigs for a fantasy novel and a nonfiction book. But our joint earnings weren't stopping the bleed. Meanwhile, the Carousel of Medical Fun kept on spinning.

It was about to discover a new gear.

In the urologist's office, I was given another blood test. Then urologist Doctor Trachmann arrived and informed me that my already high PSA had increased once again. Trachmann suggested a biopsy. Sure, why not? Go for it.

At the end of July, Trachmann went for it. A camera and some sort of snapping device were inserted up my butt. Twelve painful snaps later, tissue samples were harvested from my prostate. I left with a bleeding rectum like some prison new fish.

Nine days later, I was diagnosed with prostate cancer.

Unbelievable. I'd already had skin cancer. Wasn't there a one-cancer rule somewhere? This was early August. My health care expired at the end of September. Trachmann recommended reading a prostate cancer book and setting up another appointment. I broke the news to Joy. She was less than thrilled. But there was nowhere for us to go but ahead.

Reading up on prostate cancer, I learned that it's slow growing. An idea formed. On my next appointment, I asked Trachmann, "What if I just do nothing."

With his perpetually sad brown eyes, Trachmann said, "Then you might have ten more years to live."

I mulled that over.

Trachmann continued, "But since your cancer is borderline aggressive, the tumors could penetrate the prostate capsule, and invade the seminal vesicle or lymph nodes. Your treatment would then become more—let's just say—complicated."

Radiation and surgery remained on the table. Trachmann set up a meeting with a radiologist who explained the differences between external beam and brachytherapy radiation. I nodded like a dummy. At the same time, I met another urologist for a second opinion. I talked matters over with Joy. In the end, we settled on my getting a robotic radical prostatectomy. Or, as it's commonly known, robot surgery.

The weeks blurred. Joy raced to secure us health care beyond September. I really didn't want a McHealth Plan with another Doctor Jiffy Lube. I wanted to keep as many of my old doctors as possible. Meanwhile, I needed a pre-surgical physical, blood donations, this test, that test. (I eventually wrote a book about my experiences.)

Then surgery arrived.

I knew several men who subsequently underwent radical prostatectomy and left the hospital after a day or so. But not me. Post-op, my blood pressure cratered. A clot developed in my bladder, resulting in knife-like pains. Because of acid reflux, I could barely eat and threw everything up like an audience viewing *Battlefield Earth*. A week passed before I returned home.

Then the fun amped up.

I was incontinent, a urine hose. To tame the yellow beast became my focus throughout the fall months. Trachmann urged me to walk daily. With catheter bags and surgical drains concealed, I'd shuffle up and down the sidewalks around my building three times a day, ten minutes a session. No run/walks or chi running or peppy cadence metronomes. I felt miserable, despondent, sodden.

Working like mad, Joy secured new insurance. I lost Reznor, along with Nakamura and Weddle, plus my dentist and optometrist. Trachmann made the cut. At that moment, he was the most important of my medical friends.

Gradually, matters stabilized. I lost 35 pounds. Meanwhile, I walked doubled over as if gut punched. Standing straight put pressure on my bladder, which then voided. For Christmas, we traveled up to Seattle to visit my sister. The trip seemed to consist of scouting out the locations of the nearest washroom.

By year's end, I could stationary cycle for short periods. The once-ominous dull knee ache was gone. The neighborhood strolls continued. I could navigate from my comfy chair to the washroom without incident, provided my upper body stayed horizontal.

Thoughts of running a marathon, chi running, or running at all, were parked and forgotten.

Chapter Eight

2015

B est Picture: *Birdman*
Super Bowl Champ: New England Patriots
Billboard Hot 100 Top Single: "Uptown Funk" by Mark
Ronson ft. Bruno Mars
U.S. President: Barack H. Obama
Top Web Browser: Google Chrome

"Happiness is good health and a bad memory."

— Ingrid Bergman

The journal *Annals of Physics* reported the discovery of a supermassive black hole at the center of our galaxy. I discovered something similar in the world of health care. As the new year commenced, I blogged:

"Take a prescription to your pharmacy. Later, return for a refill; get charged full price, call the health insurance; wither on a phone tree before being shunted to a dead end; check their website and learn only FAQ questions are answered. Call back, dangle like a Christmas ornament waiting for a human. In time, you discover that refills require a document from your doctor's office. Notify the doctor's insurance gals who must have a nurse sign off on the request. Check back and learn the nurse has placed said request in the pipeline. Ten days later, the insurance approved the request. Take a prescription to your pharmacy . . ."

Our new exciting healthcare—NEH—kept us guessing as to what form of hijinks they'd pull next. For example, I needed semiannual body screens for skin cancer. As mentioned, NEH wouldn't cover Reznor with whom I'd shared many a burn and scrape. After checking the NEH website, I selected a new dermatologist and received my body screening from her. I also received a bill for full payment, thus negating the purpose of insurance. A telephone inquiry revealed that the doctor I'd seen was deemed out-of-network. I called NEH and finally reached a human.

"Seven hundred dollars? Are you serious? The doctor was listed on your website. You recommended her."

NEH: "Well, that's old information."

"Your endorsement was implicit."

NEH: "I'm sorry, but NEH doesn't cover out-of-network providers."

I contacted a small state office. The government of California does many things, some of them good. Their obscure Office of Insurance Foul-Ups provided me with courteous service, follow-ups, and prompt positive action in dealing with NEH's grotesque billing practices. Turns out I wasn't the only one suckered by the outdated NEH website. In the end, I wasn't billed. What became of the helpful woman who assisted me? She was probably fired for making other state employees look bad.

But NEH did cover Doctor Trachmann. Each visit to his office resulted in a blood test. Each blood test returned negative. I remained cancer-free. Trachmann said my prostate had been 20 percent lousy with tumors. My niece suggested I reacquire the prostate, bronze it, and offer it as a premium on a fundraising website. While admiring her spirit, I passed.

As I slowly healed, I stayed busy writing. I cranked out a parody western-romance book, then continued work on a Lovecraftian fiction project. Marketing stayed mostly fallow, though a few jobs cropped up. A nonunion animation script fell into my lap. To my surprise, I also landed a union animation script from Disney. With a weak bladder, I was grateful to be typing away behind a desk three yards away from a bathroom. Much better than, say, directing traffic.

With my weight on the rise, I returned to the Griffith Park bridle trails. I walked 2.5 miles and felt exhausted.

A single mile was about all I could handle. Through the spring and early summer, I'd walk a mile several times a week. Then I tried walking a fast mile. Spitlk. You know the rest.

As I raided the 401k on a regular basis, Joy and I brainstormed ways to earn more money. She edited a few books for independent authors. I kept working on the Lovecraft novel as our debt once again ballooned.

I celebrated Independence Day by circling the Rose Bowl. Ambling around the pedestrian ring, I watched joggers and runners weave about me like electrons around a plump nucleus. Years had passed since I'd walked a loop, and I savored the experience. I can't recall if the Coastal Oak still stood.

July 4, 2010, came to mind. The Santa Clarita 5k remained the last time I'd run a race front to back. Maybe that was all there'd be.

Existence now seemed a state where my pleasant days were mere placeholders for operations, medical procedures, and physical therapy. My stop-and-go chi running still hadn't outmaneuvered spitlk. Marathons seemed curious and distant, like recalling an era when you wore satin shirts and bell bottoms.

The first Chicago Marathon happened in September 1977. Back then it was called the Mayor Daley Marathon. I didn't run it for vague reasons. But after another year of reading *Runners World*, I was ready for the 1978 version. Checking the *Chicago Tribune*, I located the sign-up info, mailed in a couple of bucks, and received an envelope with my race bib, four safety pins, and a cotton T-shirt. I was in. Now all I had to do was train.

As with the Lakefront 10, I felt ignorance of distance running was a feature, not a drawback. The river of my youthful overconfidence knew no levee. I would simply go forth and train.

But changes had occurred since the ten-miler. I still worked at the post office and still attended junior college. But now, I was spending several nights a week performing stand-up comedy at local clubs. I'd started smoking once more, and my drinking was inching toward the semipro level. My girlfriend and I parted ways. Drinking was definitely a factor.

Before classes I'd hit the bike trails in the forest preserve. I never saw a cyclist and hardly any other runners. Birds serenaded the bap of my feet on asphalt. You'd feel a crisp bite in the air as autumn cross-faded with the damp heat of a Chicagoland summer.

A little knowledge is a dangerous thing. Knowledge poorly understood is even worse. As the marathon approached, I read about collapse point. Popular in the '70s, collapse point was a running term marking out the theoretical distance a runner's training would allow him to cover. For a marathon, a runner needed to average at least nine miles per day, or 63 miles a week. This was said to be necessary to build up endurance for 26.2. There was more to collapse point theory, but it seemed complicated and very math-like. All I remembered was collapse point and nine miles.

On my three weekly runs, I upped the mileage to nine. Twenty-seven miles a week seemed sufficient. Since a marathon was only 26.2, that left me .8 miles to spare. It all made sense if your brain was marinating in Old Style beer.

But stand-up comedy nights were becoming their own marathon. After the clubs closed, I'd join several comics who congregated at local bars out near O'Hare Airport. These sessions of liquor and mirth often lasted until the early hours. I'd drive home red-eyed, listening to Gerry Rafferty's "Baker Street."

On bleary dehydrated mornings, training runs were the first of the day's obligations tossed overboard. Psych and criminal law classes often followed. On a few occasions, work itself flew over the railing as I spent the day recovering.

Comic Jimmy Fallon once quipped, "How do you know if someone ran a marathon? Don't worry, they'll tell you." I couldn't wait for the finish line. I'd already shot off my big mouth, gabbing around how I'd kill this marathon. Fellow workers, other comics, friends and family, girls I was hitting on; if you knew me, you knew I was running the Mayor Daley Marathon.

But thanks to a packed schedule, and a love of airport drinking, my weekly mileage dropped. *I'll tough out the distance. All these miles are just padding. You don't need as much.* As race day neared, the excuses worked their way deeper into my psyche. *The distance is too much. Why try just to fail?*

I spent the night before the race drinking pitchers in a bar. I spent the morning of the marathon sleeping off the pitchers.

I'd found a new collapse point.

On a historical note, the 1978 Mayor Daly Marathon started at 10:30 AM on a day when temperatures crested 80 degrees. Runners protested about heat hazards and a mid-morning gun time—the official start time of the race. No changes were made, and off galloped nine thousand people. Temperature and humidity felled hundreds who required medical attention. Ten people were hospitalized. Chicago Mayor Michael Bilandic blamed the marathoners for being out-of-shape.

History would repeat itself.

For the next week, friends, family, and co-workers asked why I'd trained but didn't run the race. I said dumb things, made jokes, inferred it was a decision based on the temperature, and other transparent cheesy excuses. In truth, I felt ashamed over quitting. It tasted terrible. I vowed that I would nail a marathon.

And I did.

Just not that century.

In August, I ventured a few walks around the Griffith Park bridle trails. But consistent exercise diminished while I wrestled with the horror/comedy novel. I knew the ending but getting there was an odyssey. The whole middle of the book needed to be scrapped. Various story threads required reweaving; character arcs changed. In the middle of my author woes, one of the marketing guys called with a job.

Oh, boy, could we use the money.

I turned him down.

He immediately offered more money. To my surprise, I still declined. Much as I hated this book, I intended to finish. Besides, I was tired of using the written word as a sales bludgeon.

Another nonunion animated script arrived in September. A company in Singapore had requested my services. How thoughtful and kind. As things turned out, this animated script would be my last.

Joy took a seasonal position at JCPenney. Training for the Christmas season began in October. Despite the low pay, Joy felt good having a job. Around the same time, we spent a weekend up in Lake Arrowhead. We enjoyed the cool mountain air, wind in the pines, and especially the quiet.

Meantime, my overall health started sliding. Minor colds and headaches dogged me. Depression stopped by to see how I'd been. Every morning I stared at the clock, wishing it were evening already. At my desk, I munched junk food as I battled with the book.

Across the world, migrants from Syria, Iraq, and Afghanistan continued their year-long swarm into Europe. I continued my erratic physical fitness attempts into November. A solid week of cycling/walking would shrink to a single workout the next seven days. With the approach of Thanksgiving, Joy's retail job swallowed up her time.

On Thanksgiving Day, Joy's mom and I dined at a little coffee shop. We picked up a turkey dinner to-go. Back home, I popped it in the fridge and left a note for Joy. The next morning, I found the empty Styrofoam tray on the counter.

Over the Black Friday weekend, Joy's work schedule accelerated, reaching hypervelocity in December. Joy would return home late, eat, then sleep. She would arise the next day, wash up, and return to work. I missed her. I wanted to tell her that I'd finished the book.

Well, at least the first draft. As Christmas neared, I rewrote and polished. Mostly I stared at the TV, thinking of sunnier days.

Still, I remained cancer-free. I was learning to live with incontinence. I'd completed two e-books and a softcover paperback book. I'd turned down marketing work and felt fantastic. Joy and I had financially survived another year by the narrowest of margins.

Ernesto and I continued meeting for Saturday breakfast. Our discussions ranged over the San Bernardino terrorists, the rise of Donald Trump, and *Star Wars: The Force Awakens*. We talked less of the thing that once united us: running marathons. In fact, I hadn't run once that year. No chi running or walking, run/walks, or even an attempted run. I couldn't recall the last time that had happened.

Operant conditioning is a type of learning where behavior is modified by reinforcement or punishment. Spitlk had provided the punishment. I'd learned and obeyed.

After seven years, it seemed the marathon had finally secured a spot in my past.

And running had gone along for the ride.

ASCENT

Chapter Nine

2016

Best Picture: *Spotlight*
Super Bowl Champ: Denver Broncos
Billboard Hot 100 Top Single: "Love Yourself" by Justin Bieber
U.S. President: Barack H. Obama
Top Web Browser: Google Chrome

> "Failure is simply the opportunity to begin again, this time more intelligently."

— Henry Ford

A few animation scripts a year isn't a profession.

It's not even a hobby, but it does underscore the old Hollywood adage: No One Wants to Work with the Elderly. Checking around, I learned that my earned union hours were sufficient for retirement. In addition to receiving a modest monthly annuity, I would also qualify for Motion Picture Health Care. Once Medicare kicked in, Motion Picture would default to my secondary health plan. No more Carousel of Medical Fun.

Joy and I talked it over. Since leaving the retail job, she'd picked up freelance editing work for a journal specializing in transportation issues. The journal published a great deal, so Joy's position brought in steady income. Add my retirement annuity, and the money saved by not paying COBRA, and we could almost scrape by.

I filled out the retirement paperwork.

Meanwhile, fat drooped from my cheeks as if I were melting. I looked like politician Mitch McConnell. Recovering from the cancer operation, plus writing two books, plus light exercise, had landed me back in blimp town. Determined to shed pounds, I realized I needed a modest goal. So, in January, I signed up for a 5k.

I chose the Santa Anita Derby Day. Held in early April, starting and ending on the grounds of the Santa Anita Racetrack, this would be another revenge run. A decade earlier, I'd rolled a foot in mile one, breaking the 5th metatarsal. I limped across the finish line. My TNT friends would run the 2006 San Diego Marathon without me. Seven months would pass before I darkened another marathon start line.

But no goals were ventured for 2016. If I ran, great. If I walked 3.1 miles, super cool. With more enthusiasm than

I'd mustered recently, I began training. Maybe it was the desire to lose weight or the freeing thought of retirement. Whatever the case, I even reopened the chi running book.

Like collapse point 38 years earlier, I'd been cherry-picking chi running, selecting bits I could do immediately, and forsaking the whole. This time I adopted a more systemic approach. The chi running program emphasized form aspects such as staying tall with my back straight when leaning. I'd study one such form focus and practice it during weekly running sessions.

Along with stationary cycling, I walked two or three times every week. A circuit around the Wilson-Harding Golf Course was 2.5 miles. Feeling bold, I sometimes exceeded that distance, walking further south to the sound of traffic from the 5 Freeway to the east.

Because I drove a trunkless jeep, I'd carry my wallet and keys in an old fanny pack. Once at dusk, I discovered my wallet missing. It must've fallen out during the walk. Grabbing a flashlight from the jeep, I retraced my route. Nothing. As usual, there was no cash in the wallet, but there were credit cards. I imagined some coyote using my Visa to order rabbits off Amazon. I fumed and cursed and kicked things that weren't especially hard. Then I drove home and began calling credit card companies.

That same month I experimented with a two-mile run. No soreness or spitlk. But in subsequent exercise periods, I returned to walking. Push too fast and I'd injure myself and lose all momentum. No timing, no splits, no strong finishes, no run/walks. Easy does it.

As presidential primaries heated up, I sent in the retirement paperwork. Then I booked an appointment with the Motion Picture Industry Pension and Health Plan. Since 1990, I'd been writing TV animation. How strange to finally pull the ripcord. I'd had such fantastic times.

From a broke improvisational actor at the Acme Comedy Theatre, I'd landed a staff job on a popular animated series (*Animaniacs*). I'd met a famous movie director. I'd attended Beverly Hills award ceremonies in a rented tuxedo. At New York City's Radio City Music Hall, I'd stood on stage near Donny and Marie. Toward the end of my time at the studio, I traveled to Southeast Asia, part of a public service team using animation to warn of landmine dangers. (A tale worthy of its own book.)

At the start of the 21st century, my Warner Bros. contract expired. I was rolling in cash. A networking man might've called all his connections, hustled, written premises, springboards, outlines, entire shows, and not stopped until he'd landed a staff job or development deal. Many of my peers did that.

Networking seemed like begging. Instead, I sprawled on my financial cushion like a Gulf State pasha, doing only as much as I fancied. When the money drained away like cold bathwater, I sprang off my butt. But not every dead battery can be jump-started.

Now my career was over.

I felt relieved.

In March, I attempted running once more. Not far, not fast. But I moved as if crossing brittle ice. I didn't want another injury. I feared knee pain would become the fabled insanity that repeated itself, while I expected different results. After each session, I awaited spitlk like a crippled impala watching for hyenas.

While outlining a new book, I stayed busy hawking the old ones. Facebook, Twitter, Goodreads, Pinterest, and LinkedIn, all knew the blunt tone of my sales pitch. Learning iMovie, I created and posted book videos. Time was budgeted to study Google Analytics and keywords, but they bored me, so I stopped. I undertook a book giveaway on Goodreads. My horror/comedy novel was in pre-order on Kindle.

April arrived.

A life-changing event descended on our household.

But first, the Santa Anita Derby Day.

On my blog, I compared 2006 and 2016 Derby Days. Safety pins still attached race bibs to shirts. However:

No more securing a chip to your shoe with plastic strips. A timer strip was now included inside the race bib.

A mere 5k offered a technical shirt plus a finishers medal of better quality than I'd received for marathons.

A small drone circled the start line.

Compression socks were all the rage.

So were selfies taken at every stage of the race. (It's only 3.1 miles, not Badwater.)

An air horn sounded. Near the back of the pack, I leaned forward and began.

I can't say I ran the whole distance. It was more of a lumbering shuffle. The final tenth of a mile crossed the Santa Anita racetrack proper. Thanks to a recent rain, the cinder surface was a gooey quagmire. To pass anyone, you'd need to slop out into the muck and punch it. I found a tire track that offered some traction. For the first time in five years, I crossed a finish line.

Here's an odd stat. In 2006, in excellent shape, with an eight-minute first mile, I completed the race in 37:41. Ten years later, in terrible shape, I clocked a 37:36. Does being chubby beat a broken bone by five seconds? No insights here. That Saturday, I lounged around the house smiling. Joy suspected I was up to something devious.

Joy had her own reasons to smile. An electric bus company based in China had hired her full-time. The company sold different-sized electric buses to American municipal governments. Joy would be writing and editing the text of sales proposals for the firm's U.S. branch. And while her commute to a downtown LA office would be long, Joy's salary would be ample enough to support us with money left over. No more groceries on the credit card. Talk about a reprieve.

Suddenly having money was like being diagnosed with cancer. Your life has changed, but everything around you appeared the same. We'd been down so long that the financial upside seemed quirky and odd. Joy and I joked that I should've retired years ago—clearly, that's what brought good luck.

Emboldened by the 5k, I continued chi running. Some knee soreness arose in May, and I eased off. At the same time, flu-like symptoms struck me like a cinder block. Nasal congestion meant I wouldn't be sleeping. Sometimes I'd sit in front of the TV sniffling, drifting in and out of consciousness. Here is my viewing schedule from one late afternoon into the evening: *We Were Soldiers, The Hunt for Red October, Night of the Comet, In Cold Blood*—but only one hour as sleep took me.

Three weeks later, I returned to running. No timing the runs. All went well that summer. I stayed pain-free. Across the Atlantic, Britain voted for withdrawal from the European Union on the road to becoming EU-free.

At the Olympics in Rio de Janeiro, American Galen Rupp won the bronze medal. Jared Ward crossed the finish line in 6th. For the women, Shalane Flanagan also notched 6th, with fellow yanks Desiree Linden and Amy Cragg rolling in at 7th and 9th, respectively.

In September, I visited my family in Seattle. While there, I attended a chi running seminar held by founder Danny Dreyer. I picked up more insights and tips, then incorporated the various corrections into my running efforts. To my surprise, I found I was doing a few things right. But it wasn't all that astonishing. Spitlk remained my true compass. Deviate from proper chi form, backslide into heel striking, and pain would correct my ways.

By October, I'd lost 25 pounds and several inches from my waist. For the last eight months, I'd been running one to three times a week. I'd only timed myself once. Cross-training on the stationary bike had been steady, encouraged by the now Brexited Brits of Global Cycling Network.

To be safe, I reduced my runs in November and December. Mostly I confined myself to walks. Do. Not. Overdo.

Distance stayed at a three-mile ceiling. Speed remained slow. The chi running program was clear on that point: speed follows form and distance. If you could hold your form over time and distance, you could experiment with leaning more and gaining speed. Strong core muscles were a must.

Danny Dreyer referred to the angle of lean as your gears. Falling forward in first gear resulted in movement at a mild pace, second gear was training pace, third gear was race pace, and fourth was maximum effort. I could lean enough for first gear. Occasionally, I'd venture into second but couldn't hold it long. My core muscles were rather spongy.

No other races tempted me, not even 5ks. Consistent running was enough. How many years since I'd run this long without cursed spitlk? As the nation pondered the recent presidential election results, I felt encouraged. Such great changes for the household, financially and athletically.

Come 2017, I'd attempt a bit of distance.

Chapter Ten

2017

B est Picture: *Moonlight*
Super Bowl Champ: New England Patriots
Billboard Hot 100 Top Single: "Shape of You" by Ed
Sheeran
U.S. President: Donald J. Trump
Top Web Browser: Google Chrome

> "A man beaten in a marathon race can only
> look inward."

— Hal Higdon

During the mid to late '80s, I lived in Hollywood north
of Wilcox and Yucca. Located in a seedy neighborhood,
I'd later see those streets on *Cops*. Having driven out to
California in 1979, I'd tried stand-up comedy and ran out

of money. While working for a burglar alarm company, I'd switched my efforts to improvisational comedy. From audience suggestions, actors would build a scene. With a little luck, it would be a funny scene.

In 1984, I worked as a dispatcher for a messenger service. During the Olympics that year, Joan Benoit Samuelson won the first Women's Olympic Marathon. After her, no U.S. marathoner would grace an Olympic podium for a generation.

With the death of my parents, I inherited some money and decided to finish college. After classes at the University of Southern California, I'd return home to my tiny apartment above a garage. Three times a week, I'd run eight miles. Dashing across Cahuenga Boulevard, I'd run over to Ivar Avenue, then up narrow streets to Lake Hollywood. I'd zip around the reservoir alongside roller skaters, dog walkers, and skateboarders, pass atop the dam, then back downhill across Cahuenga. In the median grass near a bus stop, bearded homeless men would sleep crumpled up like Civil War dead. Back I'd dash to my apartment, celebrating another successful run with a cigarette.

Zip ahead to March 2005: I'd been off drinking and drugs for 21 years. But I still smoked. Running had ebbed. I was quite overweight, completing a six-week stint as a story editor at Disney. A certain caustic Disney executive kept the writing staff on edge. In the weekly meetings for our show about a robot cat, this executive would chuck unfavorable scripts into a wastebasket. I was too far down the organizational chart to attend. But I'd watch the producer and senior story editors spend hours in conclave. Pre-meeting, they'd discuss strategies to keep scripts out of the wastebasket. Post-meeting, they'd rehash events and what was said, how it was said, and what it all meant. They were like mice dropped into a terrarium, wondering how to please a corn snake.

Shortly before the end of my contract, I was web surfing on company time and read a story about the recent LA Marathon. I made two decisions:

I would quit smoking.

I would run next year's LA Marathon.

At home that night, filled with resolve, I stepped out the front door of our house into a chilly, wet night. After barreling down a hill for a half mile, I reversed course and stumbled home, gassed, wheezing, but resolute. I had unfinished business from 1978.

Since the next LA Marathon was eleven months off, I figured to build myself up, slowly increasing monthly mileage. Over time, my body would be trained to accept longer distances. No more snap decisions on ill-understood training methods. No more collapse point madness.

I quit cigarettes. For the next several months, I ran four or five times a week, often around the Rose Bowl. There was no time goal for training or the end-product 26.2. Finish the marathon; one and done. Bask in the glory and move on.

My sister in Tempe recommended Team in Training. (At the mention of "team," my first thought was running up and down bleachers in the gym.) Mary had completed a hundred-mile bike ride with an Arizona chapter. She felt training with people who shared your goals was a huge plus. As a loner, I found it a curious view.

Nevertheless, that August I stopped by a local library for a TNT recruitment meeting. As mentioned, in return for raising money to fight blood cancers, the team would train me up to complete an endurance event. Of the races offered, the Honolulu Marathon caught my eye.

Does it really matter what marathon I run? I thought it over. Honolulu was in December, three months before LA—less training to reach the same goal. And the team trained at the Rose Bowl. Finally, Honolulu seemed like a sweet spot for a little vacation. Before you could say "Gatorade," I'd joined TNT's San Gabriel Valley Winter Marathon Team.

At our first Saturday training session, we were tasked with running or walking three miles around the Rose Bowl. Coaches lined us up in the northwest corner of Lot K near a small Coastal Live Oak. Off we went in a herd, gradually stretching out near the first mile.

Based on my finish time of 28 minutes, I was assigned to a pace group of runners with equivalent times. Each pace group received a Galloway run/walk ratio. As mentioned, breaking up a run by walking helps with muscle fatigue, releases endorphins, and aids runners in recovering quicker. More importantly, each pace group contained the people you'd run-talk-share your life with for the next several months.

Ernesto and I took to running together in our 3x1 pace group. He was born the year I entered the Lakefront Ten. On our long runs, we discussed football, real estate, history, movies, and football. Boston CJ, out from Beantown, often joined us. In addition, there was M.I.T. Dave, a former physicist who'd worked for the government creating death rays. (At least, that's how I kidded him.) Our team veteran was Painter Jeff, a former college soccer and football player with a passion for Notre Dame football and golf.

Within two weeks, our group sported identical black Ironman sports watches with an interval timer—except Jeff who already had one. Electronic beeps became a part of life. After three minutes, little beeps would announce our walk break. A minute on, little beeps would announce run time. To this day, I can't hear a little beep without changing my speed.

On early Saturday mornings, long runs were a team event. Dawn would color the sky pink and peach above the dark San Gabriel Mountains. As our runs grew longer, we'd head south along the Arroyo Seco Channel and/or north up into the hills above the Rose Bowl. There I learned to smack the Elmer Smith sign.

One Saturday morning after a 14-mile run, I had an epiphany. I'd just set a new personal distance record. After

28 years, I'd finally surpassed running the mail drops from back in the Age of Disco.

Jimmy was our dynamic head coach. From him, we learned pacing, hydration, refueling, cross-training, and the value of hill running. He was like a contractor, teaching us all the elements necessary to build a successful house. Track practices were offered during the later weeks of training. (But no bleachers.) I stayed healthy and kept away from smoking. My run/walk increased to 4x1. My confidence swelled, then bloated. I wasn't just going to finish a marathon. I was gonna crush it like a plastic cup.

As December arrived, I received a wristband with mile splits for Honolulu. If I remained on pace, I could leave the islands a 4:59:59 finisher. As I came to understand, sub-five hours was pretty good for a rookie marathoner in his early 50s.

And then it was time.

Fireworks burst in the pre-dawn sky over the Pacific. On a steamy morning on Ala Moana Boulevard in downtown Honolulu, my marathon finally began. A Sea of Humanity race, 24,000 participants bolted-sprinted-lurched-sauntered into the early morning. Japan Airlines sponsored the event, hence 61 percent of the participants hailed from the Land of the Rising Sun.

Matters went awry at once. Two miles in, I needed to take an enormous number two. Other runners shared this and similar needs. Finding a Porta-Potty without a line wasn't easy. Finally completing my task, I hurried to recover lost time. In the humidity, I sped up, feeling as if my body were wrapped in a damp, steaming towel. My pace grew erratic, quickening as I passed foursomes of women, then slowing as the course narrowed heading up Diamond Head. Around the half-marathon mark, I felt cooked, dumping water over my head at every station.

Persistent quit thoughts arrived around mile 16. Training for Honolulu had been too easy. I'd never really been challenged. I wasn't prepared for the mental onslaught. It sounded like I had a mother in my head: *It's too hot. You're going too fast. Slow down or you'll die on the side of the road like a sick dog.*

Around mile 19, I spied a pair of purple shirts. Catching up with Ernesto and Boston CJ, we ran uphill on the Kalanianaole Highway. I stayed with them a mile. Once again, the quit thoughts swarmed.

This time they dominated.

I veered off to the side of the course. A Japanese man in a sumo outfit passed me. I walked and kept walking. Mile 21. 22.

On Kahala Avenue, heading back up toward Diamond Head, I heard clack-clack-clack-clack. A Japanese guy in wooden clogs clattered past. How could he run in those things? I tried a spot of running at 24. Joy appeared on the side of the road and waved me on. Along with my sister, Joy and Mary had been moving around the course, cheering me on. I'd wave, but my facial expression resembled a man who'd just closed a door on his thumb.

Mile 25 led uphill along a blazing naked road beside Diamond Head. To my left, the peaceful ocean filled the horizon. I wished I were floating in it. At mile 26, Coach Jimmy waved me on. I found enough gas to run the final .2 into Kapiolani Park. In the finish line photo, you can see my arms raised halfway in the air as if surrendering to the Sheriff's Department.

6:01:00

Arches, calves, and IT bands cramped or ached or both. Worse, I felt disgusted with myself. Capable of so much more, I had quit. Given up. Overcome nothing. Tossed away an opportunity like a tainted robot cat script. Something had changed. I'd finally run my marathon, but finishing below my potential felt worse than blowing off the race and drinking pitchers.

At first, I made excuses for my time. "Stepped into a pool of water and got blisters." "Didn't eat breakfast and went all light-headed." "Underhydrated early and burned out." But I stopped after the first day. The words tasted of defeat and oven-fresh lie. Worse, a man in wooden clogs had passed me and I'd let him.

The ghost of 1978 was finally laid to rest.

But the ghost of 2005 was just checking in.

I carried over my 2016 low mileage habits into the first six months of the year. Because of my latest writing project, I hardly ran in January and February. But March and April brought a return to consistency. No more than three miles a session, no timing, two or three runs a week. I'd listen to the chi running app on my phone, working to increase my awareness, lean, and cadence. Cross-training consisted mainly of Poor Man's Peloton on the stationary bike.

In May, my mother-in-law underwent open heart surgery. Hospital visits, visiting in-laws, locating a facility for mom to recover post-op ate up the days. Finally, Joy located a care facility where her mother could strengthen up before returning home. With Joy working full-time selling harmonious Chinese buses whose engines only occasionally burst into flames, I assumed the bulk of visiting duties.

I kept running. In June, I tripped and fell in Griffith Park. Landing on sunbaked, rocky ground, I fractured my left ulna. At last! A new injury! The doctors said it wasn't too bad. Rummaging around a closet, I found an old sling, rigging it so I could drive with the arm.

And kept running.

Then in July, I added a four-mile run to each week. I felt elated, excited, as if transgressing some taboo. The same low speed-no timing principles applied. I focused on the chi running form, knowing spitlk would howl if I heel struck.

My mother-in-law returned home in late summer, her health much improved. Meanwhile, I assembled notes taken during my prostate cancer days. I worked on finishing an ebook concerning that ordeal.

Joy and I were paying down the credit cards. Because of her long commute, we bought her a used SUV. In the rush hour crawl, Joy's Spotify playlists expanded. She developed a fondness for Al Stewart.

That October, I pushed a small boundary: I ran 5 miles. All went well. But once again, fires in Santa Barbara, Ventura County, LA, and San Diego threw up pyro cumulous clouds. Hundreds of thousands of acres were burned. Tens of thousands of people were evacuated. It was like living in a vast smokestack.

In November, I ventured a single six-mile run, my longest since '08. No soreness or spitlk. That month, Shalane Flanagan became the first American woman to win the New York City Marathon in 40 years.

As Christmas approached, I became anxious. In December I'd run a five-miler and two six-milers. But I kept peering over my shoulder for the bad things. Increased mileage spooked me.

Still, other than a fractured arm, I'd been running consistently for almost two years. Was I ready to start training for a—I didn't want to utter the word—a long race of some kind?

Then a vicious case of the flu struck. I was on my back for at least two weeks. But as I sniffled, sneezed, and coughed up unique bits of phlegm, I pondered matters.

Perhaps a 10k. See how I do. Maybe I should time my runs again.

My chi running form was improving. I'd remained spitlk-free. What was stopping me from faster runs and longer distances?

I'd find out.

Chapter Eleven

2018

B est Picture: *The Shape of Water*
Super Bowl Champ: Philadelphia Eagles
Billboard Hot 100 Top Single: "God's Plan" by Drake
U.S. President: Donald J. Trump
Top Web Browser: Google Chrome

> "Every bad situation is a blues song waiting to happen."

— Amy Winehouse

The virus gripped my system in a naked choke hold.
Along with high temperatures, I was hacking up cups of phlegm. And because I lacked a prostate, the deep coughs resulted in jetting urine. My sinuses were clogged worse than an LA freeway on Friday evening.

As mentioned, blocked nostrils meant little sleep. All the over-the-counter medicines were on my night table: Tylenol, Neo-Synephrine, Robitussin. The illness would ease a few days, then circle back with a vengeance. Ugly business.

Not until February was I able to exercise. Entering my third year of steady running, I now took pride in moderation. Four-mile runs continued at a leisurely pace, between 12 and 13.5 minutes a mile. In March, I experimented with a five-mile run. I returned to wearing a timing watch.

They say a goal unnamed is a dream. Perhaps. But I was never injured in a dream. Having already proved the doctors and the doubters wrong, I grew wary. Thanks to chi running, I'd risen from a spitlk grave. Why run more or faster miles? Any ghosts from the California International Marathon or Boston were well-behaved and kept to themselves. Why gamble all my winnings on farther faster?

I throttled down the mileage to 2.5- and 3-mile runs. Off came the timer watch.

As Prince Harry and Meghan Markle enjoyed a May wedding at St. George's Chapel, I continued my diminished running tempo. At the same time, Joy acquired a new boss at the Chinese bus company. He excelled at dodging blame, snide remarks, and petty vengeance. In another industry, he'd be tossing scripts into wastebaskets. This new bully boss and Joy butted heads. After hearing out both sides, one of the Chinese managers ordered Joy and Bully Boss to get along.

Pleased with the outcome, Bully Boss amped up the nasty remarks with a side order of revenge-induced over-work. Only his early departures kept Joy's life bearable. (He'd leave to go running, thus blotting a fine sport by his participation.) At home, Joy spent her evenings checking Glassdoor and Monster, seeking the proverbial greener grass.

On a Friday in late June, I returned to the Rose Bowl. Under a blue, sunny sky, renovations were taking place. All-weather exercise stations were being installed around a large field southeast of the stadium. Statues were being erected of lawyers and seven-figure donors. (I could be wrong about that.) Six-foot, chain-link construction fences crisscrossed the area.

An easy three-mile run was on the schedule. However, all morning I'd been driving around on errands. I needed a washroom.

Of course, the nearest facility was blocked off by chain-link fences. You could walk around them, but that would take a minute. At the urging of my bladder, I scaled the chain-link fence.

Going up went well.

So did most of the descending.

I hopped down the last yard. Landing on concrete, I felt a sharp pain in my RIGHT knee. I laughed. Here was a dash of irony rich as Jeff Bezos. Spit-Rick, brother-of-Spit-Lick.

Five minutes later, I set out running. Spit-Rick persisted. I walked the three miles. No big deal. I'd head home, ice, rest over the weekend, then resume running. Been there, done that to the 10th power.

I guessed

In his book *On the Run from Dogs and People* author Hal Higdon observed that marathon runners "... keep seeking that one perfect race. We rarely find it."

I was destined to come close in leafy Oregon.

First, to back up a bit, after finishing Phoenix in 2007, Kate and Katie and some of the other coaches encouraged me to aim at breaking four hours. That January, I felt strong and confident. An October race would give me ample time to train. And what more fitting race than the Chicago Marathon? 2007 would mark the event's 30th running, and the 29th year since I'd weaseled out. I jumped online and signed up. Chicago would be the zenith of revenge races.

But sometimes, too long to train is as bad as not enough time. My race plan was muddled. I'd tried to do too much, mixing elements from different marathon plans. A torn calf muscle threw off my schedule. By August, it was clear

I wouldn't break four hours. My goals grew modest. Perhaps a 4:45:00 finish.

And then it was October, and I stood behind a tree in Grant Park.

Pre-race, long lines marked the Porta-Potties. Men found relief behind the trees, women behind a long hedge where I watched their heads popping up like meerkats. Over Lake Michigan, the sun rose like a nuclear fireball. In the early morning, the temperature was already 72 degrees with a cloying 83 percent humidity. A real Sea of Humanity marathon, Chicago crammed 36,000 runners into its corrals. Packed together with that many people was like sharing a sauna with everyone in Monrovia, California.

Up ahead, I saw a ripple in the mass of runners. I scuffled forward for minutes before crossing the timing mat. The official start of the race, when East Africans and other fast people tear off, was known as gun time. Because of the chip timer secured to my shoe, the instant I touched the mat became my chip time. My marathon would be measured from that moment to whenever I crossed the finish line.

My body was already damp with sweat.

By the first aid station, I knew there'd be trouble.

The water was gone. A carpet of empty plastic cups lay around the tables. I wore a belt holding a 20-ounce bottle of Gatorade. However, many runners relied solely on the aid stations for fluids.

At the 10k point, I heard the wail of sirens as the first ambulances carted off heat casualties. At some aid stations, there'd be half cups of water. Others were drier than a tax document. Runners slowed, then walked.

At the ten-mile mark, marathoners sat on the curb with glazed looks. By now, the temperature had risen another eleven degrees. In some of Chicago's concrete canyons, it felt like running through a magma chamber. My new goal was to finish the marathon. That soon changed to finish the marathon without an ambulance ride.

Police barricades appeared at the halfway point around Adams and Halsted. Cops blocked the course. The race had been canceled. Runners who arrived at the barricades were directed east toward Grant Park. Runners who'd already passed that point were in limbo. (No mention was made of refunds.)

Having already passed the barricades, lacking official guidance, I and thousands of others continued toward the finish line. Cops and EMTs called out updated information. One cop said no one would receive a finishers medal. That ticked me off. All this and no medal.

Runners continued dropping out. It was no longer a marathon but a march of thirsty people with race bibs. The bystanders were great. From corner grocery stores, people would buy a case of water and pass out the bottles. The kindness of strangers hydrated me to the finish.

There I discovered an unexpected traffic jam. Runners who'd been redirected at the barricades ran back out onto the course across the timing mat and into the path of runners finishing the marathon. The redirected then turned around and trotted a dozen yards back across the timing mat to snag a finish line photo. A chaotic ending to a wild day.

5:48:43.

As Coach Jimmy used to say, there's your training, then there's race day. My training sucked and the race had been canceled. But I did receive a finishers medal—not as elaborate as the 2016 Santa Anita Derby Days 5k, but a memento, nevertheless.

Next day the race director blamed runners for the water shortages, claiming too many poured an extra cup over their heads. The media noted that Mr. Race Director couldn't get through his own press conference without sipping from a water bottle. Cousin Mary Ann sent me a popular T-shirt that read: "The Chicago Marathon: The race quit, but I didn't."

Back in LA, over lunch, I recapped the event for Coach Katie. She mentioned a race unknown to me.

"You should try the Eugene Marathon. A friend just ran it and did pretty good."

"Eugene, huh? No kidding. Where's that?"

From the baked rubble of Chicago would come my finest marathon hour.

A week after the Rose Bowl fence incident, I tried running and backed off. Right knee pain; unbelievable. After icing and resting, I rode my stationary bike and iced some more. Then I tried another run. More right knee pain. I thought of Nakamura. But he would recommend an x-ray, then refer me to the orthopedist. Weddle would arrive after an hour, poke and prod, listen for another twenty minutes, then suggest physical therapy. I didn't want to consider an MRI. What if I now had a pothole in the right knee?

The abrupt halt to my running coincided with a writing crisis.

Returning to short stories, I'd begun a tale about a succubus in Hollywood attracted to a young director. Then I lost all confidence. I'd finish a draft, then start a new one where I'd explore interesting characters who didn't move the story forward. Then I'd start over. It was maddening. I couldn't get a handle on the process. I wanted to park the story and open a new project. But the last three years had seen a half dozen projects, opened, parked, and abandoned. I wasn't adding to the pile until I figured out why I was stuck in neutral.

Through the summer and into late September, my dejection grew alongside my appetite. How could I improve so much over the last few years and then wreck it by hopping off a fence?

Stepping on a scale, I stared down at 270 pounds. I was an amoeba. Perhaps a goal unwritten really was a dream. I chose a goal: the Pasadena Rose Bowl 5k. Scheduled for

January 2019, the race would circle the complex, finishing inside the famous stadium. It would be a veritable training run—or slow walk. To celebrate my decision, I walked a mile without pain.

Eleven years after the Chicago Marathon, Joy and I sailed to Catalina Island. We enjoyed Avalon, watching sailing ships bob in the harbor. We took a jeep tour of the island, observing the buffalo milling around like TSA employees.

Upon returning home, I dusted off some old notes. One writing project I could tackle was publishing the softcover edition of my prostate book. With Joy's help, we tinkered with formatting in preparation for a Christmas launch.

Early November brought my spouse a double shot of good news. Joy watched in delight as Bully Boss packed up his office. Surrounded by security, he was escorted from the premises. The Chinese kept things quiet. Clearly, when the Sons of the Sacred Earth were vexed, they moved with divine speed. *Sic transit*, Bully Boss. For reasons unknown, he was gone. The why of it remained opaque, like the fate of Aaron and his blue circles or the trigger of Kim's awesome cackle.

In addition, Joy's job quest had paid off with an offer from a proposal writing company ten minutes from our place. For more money and a professional work environment, Joy would start in January. She immediately set out to upgrade her work wardrobe.

A brief November run put me back on the board. A week later, I walked around the Rose Bowl, marking my first three-miler since the fence-climbing affair. I had minor soreness in the left knee, but my right knee seemed healed enough for walking.

Reviewing my running history, I once again prepared a schedule for the next year. I'd been treating 5ks as one-and-dones: 2010. 2011. 2016. Should I emerge injury-free from the January race, I'd make 5ks a regular feature. They could serve as check-ins for my progress. What I really craved was my former easy two-and-a-half years of chi running.

Before Christmas, we launched the softcover version of my prostate cancer book. Up north, Paradise, California, burned to the ground thanks to a malfunctioning power line. I viewed the upcoming year with some hope and a heavy dollop of resignation. Injury and recovery were the last things I wanted.

After all these years, they left a sour taste.

Chapter Twelve

2019

B est Picture: *Green Book*
Super Bowl Champ: New England Patriots
Billboard Hot 100 Top Single: "Old Town Road" by Lil
Nas X
U.S. President: Donald J. Trump
Top Web Browser: Google Chrome

> "You have to forget your last marathon before
> you try another."

—Frank Shorter

Virginia was a Team in Training mission captain.

She reminded participants of the havoc blood cancers unleashed upon patients and their families. She provided updates on the scientific progress being made by TNT fundraising. Along with her husband Van, Virginia walked races, cheered on participants, encouraged, and supported the team. Cancer survivors Van and Virginia were the heart of the San Gabriel Valley Marathon Team. (Or, at least, a large aorta.)

On a chilly January morning, I bumped into Virginia at the Rose Bowl 5k. We shivered together in the gloomy winter air, waiting for the air horn. Alongside Virginia were M.I.T Dave and several other current and former TNTers. Virginia was feeling poorly that day and planned to take her time.

Our chat ended as the pack surged forward. Off I rumbled on my first race since Santa Anita 2016. Around the Rose Bowl, I went with the speed of an elephant seal on a gravel road. Entering the stadium, I finally ran but was picked off at the finish line by a 12-year-old boy.

Beyond the timing mat were photographers and bling. Past that were booths offering post-race bananas and bagels, orange slices, and plastic bottles of water. I logged a 43:40, dead center amidst twelve men in my age group. Considering my miserable shape, a sixth-place age-group finish was quite a coup.

In order to run consistently that year, I planned to walk first, then mix walks and runs, then return to running three times a week. To stay motivated, I'd added three more 5ks. Paying money to run would aid focus.

The next two months saw lots of walking and GCN cycling. A bit of running, but not much. On the writing front, my story constipation vanished. Last year's horror tale was wrapped up and sent out. More short stories suggested themselves. Enjoyment returned to fiction writing.

For marketing reasons, I decided to build my own website. My tech skills equaled my marathon-savvy in the '70s, animation writing in the early '90s, and copywriting in the '10s. But ignorance never stopped a determined man.

At least two hours a day were dedicated to domain names, hosting services, software, drag-n-drop page builders. Every element begged a new question that required research. After a short time, it all grew tedious, like watching YouTube to learn optical surgery. At a certain point, the venture had devoured too much effort and money to be outsourced. I believe that's called the Sunk Cost Fallacy. Yet, on I went. Or, as cartoonist Walt Kelly once wrote, "Having lost sight of our objectives, we redoubled our efforts."

As Joy commenced her new job down the street, she discovered the company encouraged physical fitness. Various corporate branches engaged in walking competitions. Joy began walking on her breaks. She decided to up her game and buy new athletic shoes.

In April, we visited Run With Us in Pasadena, an old TNT haunt. (That's where the '05 team purchased all their Ironman watches.) Joy selected a pair of shoes, and so did I, not having bought running shoes—or any kind of shoes—in years. The sales guy measured my feet. To my astonishment, they'd grown two inches. Like goldfish released into a lake, feet grow as you age. Ligaments and tendons lose elasticity over time. And if you're over-weight, that's additional pressure on the arch, causing it to lengthen. Fortunately, jumbo Brooks running shoes were in stock.

Three weeks later, I was stretching out in Griffith Park when Boston CJ ran past. He'd been running the bridle trails lately and alerted me to a good four-mile loop. We chatted briefly. He was tending bar in a new restaurant and asked after Ernesto. Then off he went. We'd meet again on the trails.

In June, there was a party at the Rose Bowl.

Once Virginia had suffered from chronic myelogenous leukemia (CML) and her future seemed abridged. But thanks to Leukemia and Lymphoma funding, Virginia had received a second chance, courtesy of a drug called Gleevec. No more nausea, blood transfusions, or killer infections. Gleevec once a day kept the cancer at bay. Following a Saturday practice, Virginia would be celebrating her 20th year of Gleevec-enabled existence. Ernesto and I dropped by.

This was a very nostalgic morning with the team. Ultra-runner Coach Kiley arrived along with English Caroline, M.I.T Dave, and, of course, Van and Virginia. It was nice to mingle with runners, listen to their training woes and goals, and share tales of races past.

Under an overcast sky, inquiries were made about my chi running and whether I was training for anything. My glibness was in full swing. I mentioned I had an excellent book title and needed to run one more marathon to ensure a happy ending. (The joke title was *From Marathon to Couch Potato and Back*.) I added that my finishing time was immaterial. The team had plenty of suggestions: the LA Marathon, Long Beach, Santa Clarita. All were well-established local races.

Van is a Southern California racing database. If he hasn't walked a race, he's cheered on someone participating. Van suggested Ventura, a popular Boston Marathon qualifier. Starting in Ojai, a city of local art and pot stores, the marathon course followed paved paths descending to the coast. I liked point-to-point marathons: you never pass the same landmark twice and all the real fast people are up front somewhere.

"It's literally downhill," said Van.

My spine tingled like a mouse munching on wiring. If finishing time didn't matter, could I handle a gravity-friendly 26.2? Driving home later, I laughed. A marathon, right. Next, I'd be figuring out my collapse point.

But over the following weeks, long dormant thoughts arose, coughed, complained of the cold floor, and wandered around the kitchen of my mind, seeking the tea kettle. No marathon was a slam dunk, but a downhill run to the coast seemed possible. Of course, marathon dreams had roamed my mind before and were usually followed by major surgery.

At that moment, I wasn't even running 15 miles a month. Forgetting speed, I'd still need to train up my body to handle long distance pounding. That'd meant, at some point, running over 100 miles a month. Crazy. Impossible. I'd be injured long before I reached double-digit runs.

My vexing website finally went live. Across the Pacific in Hong Kong, protests erupted against the Chinese Communist government. Back across the Pacific in California, I added up my June mileage: 30 miles. Delighted, I scheduled four-mile runs for the next month.

And once again raced Santa Clarita.

With temperatures in the mid-60s, July 4th was overcast. Fine running weather. I'd slept poorly the previous night, didn't want to go, then thought about just walking the 3.1 miles. But I ran anyway, alongside runners listening to their splits on smartphones. I finished as an ambulance whooped past me, bound for some distressed athlete. I'd knocked seven minutes from my Pasadena time and felt glad I'd climbed out of bed.

After a 40-mile July, the marathon idea was still sleeping on my mental couch. I decided to *announce* another marathon on social media, placing wriggle room between word and deed. Still, I enjoyed including "me," "marathon," and "run" in the same sentence. Posting my goal on Facebook drew many Likes, plus a straightforward, "You aren't going to make it."

I'd already considered that.

What was so perfect about the 2008 Eugene Marathon?

For one thing, the weather: sunny, clear, and mild. And my preparation rocked. Starting in the fall of 2007, I quickly rebuilt my mileage base to 25 miles a week. I slotted in workouts to run at marathon pace. And I did nothing stupid to cause an injury. No sloping walls or leaks in the roof. This house was going up right.

Coach Kate looked over my training plan. I would maintain a 7x1 run/walk until mile 18, then shift to 8x1. Hit the half marathon point in under two hours. Drop the run/walk at mile 23. Kate suggested scheduling two twenty-mile training runs. That was stepping things up, but I managed to schedule a second twenty.

Doubt lurked like a mugger in an alley. *Don't be so hardass. Just say you want to come close to sub-four. Give yourself space in case you stink up the course.* I worked on my mental game. The conditional tense became something to avoid. If I said, "I'm trying for a sub-four," I'd correct myself to, "I'm breaking four." The same rules applied to my thoughts. Doubt never left, but I made its job tougher.

Visualizations and affirmations played their part. What clicked best was a 3x5 card taped to my computer. In Magic Marker, I'd written my finish time: 3:59:59. I would think of the time at odd moments, in line at the grocery store, driving, running, or just before sleep.

Following Kate's suggestion, I logged a 21-mile run, recovered for a month, then ran 22. The last two miles were in the eight-minute range. In April 2008, I tapered, easing off the mileage and giving my body a two-week rest.

In early May, Joy and I flew into Portland, then drove south to Eugene. At our motel, I logged online and read an email from Kate: ". . . you are totally going to rock it. Make sure to hydrate, take your salt, get rest, and think only positive thoughts!"

We drove segments of the racecourse. A few hills here and there but nothing stark. The course was a net downhill. Recalling the flatness of Phoenix, I considered a little terrain variation just fine. The half-marathon point and mile 18 seemed accessible spots for Joy to meet me.

Back in the room, I laid out my gear and then called Kate and Jimmy. While I was planning to break four hours, Jimmy was working on breaking three. I still have my notes from that call: *Be patient – stay on pace – even at 13.1 – 1:59:59 – good at 13 – pick up slightly.* Jimmy suggested that when the pain increased, I tell myself, "This is what it feels like to break four."

Another restless night, another morning when I didn't want to get up. I ate a small bowl of oatmeal and drank a 16-ounce bottle of water. Near Hayward Field, on the University of Oregon campus, the race day temperature hovered in the 40s. Joy dropped me off. I wanted to climb back in the car. After turning in my gear, I warmed up, then warmed up again alongside a mere 1,800 other runners. (And that included a pilot fish half-marathon.)

The air horn sounded.

Uphill at first, then down, then down more, then back up a long hill. I slowed, keeping my heart rate steady on the uphills. Then back through the University of Oregon campus. We crossed a wobbly wooden bridge over the Willamette River.

At the halfway point, I assessed: 1:56:52, about an 8:55 pace. A bit fast, but no strain. I decided to hold the pace a little longer. Joy cheered and took pictures. We parted with a date for mile 18. I was a marathon machine.

Good God, could it be this easy? Where was the four-hour pace group? Somewhere behind me. Ha. Handing Joy my water belt at 18, I was still two or three minutes ahead of pace. I sensed my last miles would be solid. I upped the run/walk to 8x1. Joy would meet me at the finish outside Autzen Stadium.

Like distant thunder, I noticed a heaviness building in my legs.

Across the Willamette again on a different bridge. Three hours into the race, I hit mile 20. Ample time, though my pace had dropped off and my legs felt as limber as dock pilings.

By mile 22, I was seriously leaking time. To maintain pace felt like racing through dream molasses. The four-hour pace group passed me in a burst.

Runners were breaking down from going out too fast, old injuries, or some version of the Wall where the body has drawn off glycogen stored in the muscles and is burning fat, a most unpleasant sensation. A few people stretched, others cramped; one guy staggered off the course and heaved up his guts. I sympathized.

Mile 23 saw me drop the run/walks. Eating a handful of gummy bears, I forced myself to pick up the pace. My IT bands felt like iron ingots. To distract myself, I focused on picking off racers. Locking my eyes on a runner's back, I'd pass, then lock my eyes on another. One or two caught me later, but they were probably doing the same thing.

At Autzen Stadium, Joy yelled as I traveled the final .2. An orange snow fence lined the last hundred meters. Race clock, red LED numbers, a passing runner—all became a blur. My head was tilted up, sucking air.

On the race clock, red LED numbers flashed 4:02.

I crossed the timing mat.

With my finisher's medal, space blanket, and bottle of water, I let Joy guide me to a nearby curb. I plopped down. According to my Ironman, I'd made it. Photos show me waving with a weary smile. But I kept checking the watch. What if I blew it? What if 4:02 was chip time? Such doubts result from an absence of cranial blood.

From a nearby booth, race personnel were presenting runners a readout with their official finishing time. Joy guided me over. A moment later, I clutched a paper in my sweaty hands.

3:59:53.

And the best was yet to come.

August brought another race on familiar ground. This 5k course followed some of my training runs on the Griffith Park bridle trails. Alas, this race was awash with dogs on leashes and strollers. A few festive Hawaiian shirts were visible in keeping with the race's luau theme. A woman pushing a stroller and chatting on a cell phone passed me at mile three. I pursued. From countless hours in the park, I knew the trail ahead. I'd be running on loose soil.

Keeping my quarry in sight, I waited until her stroller wheels skewed sideways in the dirt. Then I surged. But the woman lowered her phone and concentrated. Her stroller wheels found traction on harder soil. She kicked. Finish line in sight, my chi running form collapsed. Pounding ahead on my heels, I aced her out. But something more than a finisher's medal awaited.

Spitlk.

You fat half-wit.

That and other arch remarks circled my consciousness. I'd blown a promising recovery from last year's stupid injury in order to pass a stroller and acquire another stupid injury. Worse, I may have fouled up a shot at running another marathon.

A tense week passed while I stationary cycled and walked. No soreness or pain. I ventured a few short runs the following week. A little soreness, but nothing bad. I slowly added distance. Returning to form in October, I added more four-mile runs, logging a 45-mile month.

Joy and I then ran the Surfers Point 5k. From a very cold Ventura beach, the course led up a hill, then back down. Van once said that if you raced long enough, you'd start collecting age-group bling. On that brisk November morning, I ran my best time of the year, collecting my first age-group medal. Van the Man knew his stuff.

Surfers Point Marathon might be a good 26.2. Small field, cool coastal weather, scenic views. With a course labeled flat and fast, Surfers Point seemed just right for distance running. No steam bath runs like Honolulu and Chicago or polar Phoenix.

In my head, I leased space to the Surfers Point Marathon.

Five and six-mile runs marked December. Cross-training consisted of weightlifting and stationary cycling. I'd lost forty pounds that year and needed a new belt.

I sensed a marathon.

And the short story I'd once agonized over was published in an anthology.

A new decade, 2020, Olympics, and presidential election perched on the horizon.

I felt it would be my year.

Chapter Thirteen

2020

B est Picture: *Parasite*
    Super Bowl Champ: Kansas City Chiefs
Billboard Hot 100 Top Single: "Blinding Lights" by The Weekend
  U.S. President: Donald J. Trump
  Top Web Browser: Google Chrome

"You live and learn. At any rate, you live."

— Douglas Adams

Something called the Wuhan Virus or COVID-19 dominated the media. The virus came from either a wet market or a Chinese germ warfare lab, then only a wet market, then possibly a germ warfare lab.

Yeah, yeah, whatever.

I'd started the year ablaze. Weights, cycling, steady running, including my first seven-miler in years. I also notched another age group medal at January's Pasadena 5k. At 33:48, it was my best finishing time in a decade. Feeling fit and bold, I signed up for another 5k in March as well as a 10k run in Ventura that May. This would mark my first 6.2-mile race since 2008.

Unable to resist, I surfed over to MarathonGuide.com and clicked a race predictor. The predictor took a finishing time at one distance and projected it across other distances. I entered my most recent 5k time from Pasadena. According to the algorithm, I could complete a marathon in 5:28:46.

At my age and in my condition, 12:32 minutes a mile didn't seem unreasonable. True, these were only projections, but I'd used them back in the day on other races. My finishing times hadn't been far off.

Race planning intensified. A solid May 10k finish would convince me to boost my weekly mileage. The next goal would be a half-marathon. Based on the half, I'd know if I was ready for 26.2. With care and a bit of luck, I could be at the start line of Surfers Point in November.

Last June, I'd been content to finish 26.2, regardless of time. Now I craved a very specific sub-5:30. And from a race among races, Surfers Point had morphed into the ONE. I needed to chill, keep it steady. I took a deep breath. A decent 5k did not a marathon make. Nevertheless, I selected a fuchsia 3x5 card. In Magic Marker, I wrote: 5:29:59 and taped it onto my computer.

On the health front, my right shoulder felt fine. Reznor checked my skin every six months. A few sections were biopsied, but no cancer. In prostate world, my PSA stayed zero. However, my optometrist warned me about my cataracts. He suggested I act soon. But since my vision remained unclouded, I marched on.

In early February, I drove to Santa Monica for a class with chi running's Danny Dreyer. I worked on form, practiced the one-legged posture stance, and experimented with moving from my center. Breathing through my nose while running still eluded me. It released serotonin but felt like I was running under the sea.

I covered 52 miles that month. Two of my weekly long runs were seven milers. Another run was my first eight-miler since 2008. Once again, I dashed under the 210 Freeway, up a hill, under a street, past a dam, across a floodplain, beyond the Jet Propulsion Laboratories, up another hill, and finally doubling back at a triangle-shaped bridge in the foothills of the Angeles National Forest. Such confidence.

I'm coming for you, Elmer Smith Bridge.

Get ready, Mr. Marathon.

Two days later, I fell.

Around my place, there's one street with a small patch of asphalt sticking up like a ridge. Running one afternoon, I tripped over it. Falling, I managed a half-roll but shredded my left palm and knee. Keys fell out of my shorts. An SUV turned onto the street. The driver must've been from out of town since she stopped. More embarrassed than not, I gathered up my keys and dignity and finished the run.

The next day, pain gripped my lower back. No running. I iced the lumbar vertebrae. Weightlifting went on hold, and I walked. Gradually, the back pain retreated. Why was I always getting injured? Did I love self-pity and victim-hood? (Well, yes.)

Then an email arrived. My March 5k in Balboa Park was canceled.

COVID was here.

"You can make a million dollars and lose it. But run a marathon, and it's preserved for-ever, mentally and physically. . . . You'll al-ways remember the drama, the will to finish, the hard work, the determination, your race plans, and the execution of them."

Hal Higdon quotes a runner named Vince Fandetti say-ing those words a half century ago. Fandetti's words remain true. I wish they weren't. Maybe I wouldn't be tumbling in the street like a blind circus performer.

I remembered each of my five marathons. Like children raised in the same home, they had similarities but were unique. No one would be exactly like the other. That included the San Diego Rock 'n' Roll Marathon.

In June 2008, a month after my Eugene triumph, Ernesto, Boston CJ, and I drove to San Diego. (A spirited man, CJ had chosen to run the marathon dressed as Elvis.) Coaches Katie and Kate, M.I.T Dave, English Caroline, Van, and Virginia were also present. It would be my penultimate team.

As an assistant coach, I'd be inside the marathon, running alongside our participants, "sweeping" them past cut-off points and across the finish line. Under a fine marine layer, the race began. All went well for the first 13.1 miles. The other coaches and I shepherded participants past the half-marathon cut-off point. A second cut-off point was coming up at mile 19. Miss that one and you'd be bussed to the finish line at Point Loma.

I caught up with Natasha at mile 17. In a race, old injuries sometimes cropped back up. Having banged up an IT band during training, Natasha was hobbling along a bike path. A young actress, she possessed a sly sense of humor. Natasha remarked that her name spelled backwards was Ah, Satan. Despite the injury, Natasha was determined to finish. We hustled past the second cut-off point with minutes to spare.

Stopping at the next aid station, Natasha had her IT band wrapped in an ice bag and secured with duct tape. Moving up a highway bridge a mile later, the duct tape unraveled. A blind woman in a race bib passed us, tapping the curb and pavement with her cane like a woodpecker.

Around mile 21, the course veered onto a dirt road. The dirt road curved along some Mission Bay tidal inlet that smelled like an enormous bait box. By now the marine layer had burned off. It was a sunny afternoon. Since 6:30 that morning, I'd been dashing back and forth between participants. I'd already racked up well over 30 miles. I really wanted to sit. Natasha gritted her teeth in IT pain. She looked like an attractive piranha.

Traveling in the wake of a marathon is like following a retreating army: there's nothing around but trash and the wounded. Garbage everywhere, discarded cups from deserted water stations, scaffolding from bands that had long ago split for the shade. Runners limped, cursed, and walked backwards. Fortunately for Natasha and me, other TNT coaches were around to bring us water and more ice.

Two miles later, we passed the blind woman, a tapping entity, a metronome. Back on the pavement, a street sweeping machine pursued us, sucking up flattened cups. We passed under a freeway and out again into the sun.

The blind woman tapped by.

At mile 25, jets roared overhead from San Diego International Airport. The Marine Corps Recruit Depot stood on our left. Inside the base lay the marathon finish line.

Thirty-six years earlier, I'd been hounded off a bus onto that very base, stood on yellow footprints, and wondered what had possessed me to volunteer.

With the end in sight, Natasha vowed she wasn't finishing behind a blind woman. We ran, passing the tapping machine. We also passed two chicks in grass skirts and a guy wearing an "I Wish I Weren't Here" T-shirt.

7:28:30.

That night, Natasha, Ernesto, Boston CJ, and many of the other coaches and teammates went out partying. I slept instead. I'd set a personal record for most miles run in a single day. Being on the coaching clock, I considered my finishing time incidental. Besides, greater events loomed ahead. Two weeks later, I signed up for the California International Marathon. Beyond lay Boston.

At no point did I think I'd completed my last marathon.

In March, the City of Los Angeles closed Griffith Park to all athletic activity.

The City of Pasadena closed the Rose Bowl.

The County of Los Angeles closed the trails above JPL.

Fine. I'd run around my neighborhood, being mindful of jagged asphalt. Besides, it was only two weeks to "flatten the curve."

In April, Joy's job followed the state's mercurial guidelines and sent employees home. In the grocery stores, toilet paper and paper towels were rationed. Our local supermarket pasted social-distancing footprint circles on the floor telling everyone where to stand just like boot camp. Running slowed as my back still ached.

Lockdowns are creepy. Small businesses that I'd patronized for decades were shuttered. My barber shop was run by Vietnamese immigrants. Sunee was my age with two daughters. He'd escaped South Vietnam on the carrier *Midway*. Sadly, powerful politicians didn't get their haircuts at Sunee's shop. The business never reopened.

May brought the cancellation of my 10k. In three months, my motivation had gone from Everest-like heights to flatline. Progress, injury, start again, lockdown. Why bother? Surfers Point would probably be canceled.

In late May, we turned on the TV and watched Santa Monica stores being looted. Police stood around like parking meters. Nothing stops looting quicker than inert cops.

Joy's company furloughed several employees. Joy was kept on, but her salary was cut by 20 percent. Unlike many, she still had a job.

Even though Griffith Park reopened, it was tough dragging myself over there. With people laid off and schools closed, the trails were jammed. Every day was Saturday morning. Runners, walkers, strollers, and dogs on twenty-foot leashes packed the bridle trails. Most people wore masks. Some even wore masks while running. I questioned the wisdom of exhaling carbon dioxide back into one's face. You're expelling it for a reason.

This COVID business wouldn't last forever. Perhaps my running year could still be salvaged. Of course, there were always virtual races. Runners competed via the honor system. You signed up online, paid an entrance fee, ran on your own, then sent in your finishing time. In return, you were mailed a finisher medal and technical shirt. I was tempted to enter one and report I'd run a 5k in ten minutes.

The Rose Bowl reopened, and my back gradually healed. June and July were running-rich months. I resumed February's tempo. Once again, I caught myself customizing the chi running form. Back to basics. Fortunately, no spitlk. With California banning all outdoor sporting events, save mass demonstrations and rioting, Surfers Point was officially canceled.

On my blog, I stated I would continue training, then invite witnesses to watch me circle the Rose Bowl for the requisite 26.2 miles. Big talk. No one would show up for such a sterile event, including me.

Cataracts finally announced themselves. At first, I kept cleaning my eyeglasses. Then, at night, everything looked opaque. My vision developed a full-time milky blur. Much as I recoiled from the idea, I needed another operation. I made the appropriate calls.

In August, unable to eat a sit-down meal in lock-down crazy California, Joy and I drove to Arizona. Joy's job had recently restored her full salary and we were itching to celebrate. We enjoyed the cooler air of Flagstaff and the broiling heat of the Petrified Forest, not to mention the beauty of the Grand Canyon. We sat down inside an air-conditioned restaurant for Italian food. An unmasked barber cut my hair. I even ran a few miles. Then we drove through Kingman back toward the once-Golden State. Needles broiled in 115-degree heat. Through Barstow and down, we motored into lockdown land. Time away from California boosted our morale.

In the international arena, American Molly Seidel won bronze at the Tokyo Olympics. Fighting through 86 percent humidity and temperatures above 100 degrees, Seidel hung tough. She finished behind two top East African runners. Fortunately for Seidel, the Olympic Marathon wasn't organized by anyone from the Chicago Marathon. They'd have shut down the race and blamed her.

The lockdowns were a grind, but the canceling of Surfers Point punctured my zeal, triggering motivational leakage. I considered signing up for the Mesa Marathon, but days slid past without any action. Two weeks produced zero running or cross-training activity.

On the fiction front, I was writing and assembling a collection of short stories. Cancer had sidelined this project in 2014. By Christmas, I intended to publish an e-book on Amazon and Draft2Digital. I also wanted reviews in place before publication. But because of rewrites, my deadline appeared doubtful.

In the unlooted portion of Beverly Hills, I had my eye surgery. Fast, easy, and suddenly I could see quite well. After a few days, blues and whites turned up everywhere. According to the doctor, my yellowish cataracts had blocked those bands in the spectrum. In addition, I'd paid out-of-pocket for special lens that eliminated farsightedness. Fancy new eyes. Were it possible for eyes to swagger, mine would have done so.

September saw a return to running and exercise. Having an actual marathon ascending after all these years, then seeing it vanish made all the stress and struggle pointless. The goal time on my fuchsia 3x5 card seemed as worthless as a finishing time for walking to Tahiti.

I signed up for a 10k in Mesa, Arizona the following February. At least it wouldn't be canceled. Sensing another visit from my buddies, depression and weight gain, I took action.

Despite my earlier wry remarks, Joy and I entered a virtual event. The Catalina Island Run was a hundred-miler lasting from October 1 to December 31. A website tracked your progress across the island, logged times and elevation, and compared you to other participants. Complete the distance and you won a race shirt and bling. We laughed and gave it a go.

For six weeks, Joy walked, and I ran. My four-mile runs were logged onto the Catalina web page, then five milers, then a six. Soon I was running and cross-training with passion. By mid-November, I'd covered 66 virtual miles and felt my old confidence return. But for some weird reason, I decided to again customize chi running. I felt my heels weren't lifting high enough. They needed a boost.

A week of yanking heels up with every step left me with sore ligaments and tendons. I walked, tried a run, but locomotion hurt. I was finished for the rest of the year. Nothing to do but work on the front and back matter of my short-story book.

I also considered writing the *Sisyphus Guide to Marathon Training*.

A sad possibility clung to me like moist garments: Perhaps San Diego really had been my last marathon.

Chapter Fourteen

2021

B est Picture: *Coda*
Super Bowl Champ: Tampa Bay Buccaneers
Billboard Hot 100 Top Single: "Levitating" by Dua Lipa
U.S. President: Joseph R. Biden
Top Web Browser: Google Chrome

"Dreaming men are haunted men."

— Stephen Vincent Benet

At one time, you heard the phrase "runner's high" a lot. It refers to a relaxing state of euphoria caused by the release of endorphins after exercise. However, David Linden, a professor of neuroscience at Johns Hopkins, has another take. He believes the euphoria is caused by a biochemical substance called endocannabinoids. A neuromodulator similar to cannabis, but less expensive, they improve your mood, generating psychoactive effects such as reduced anxiety and calm.

I usually experience "runner's okay," whereby I feel good after running but not especially joyful. The euphoric state is rare for me. Over the years, there were four occasions worthy of the label runner's high. Two followed the '07 Phoenix Marathon and the '10 Santa Clarita 5k.

A third episode had occurred the prior February. I'd just run seven miles for the first time in years. At Griffith Park, while stretching post-run, a golfer shanked his shot onto the bridle trails. A chain link fence separates trails from the golf course. In a snarky, mocking tone loud enough for his foursome to hear, the golfer asked me to fetch his ball. I ignored him. He erupted in rage, cursed, wished me ill, and threatened a golf club attack. But I was unflustered, awash in endocannabinoid-induced euphoria. Perched atop a towering crag of peace, I finished stretching and strolled off, leaving the golfer railing like a scalded ape.

On each of those three occasions, the runner's high evaporated in an hour or two.

But not after the 2008 Eugene Marathon.

From crossing the finish line in the late morning until the following Thursday, I was awash in a blissful state of calm. Post-race, I took an ice bath, lounged around with Joy, called Kate and Jimmy, ate, tossed up a victory post on my blog, ate, then had dinner. No matter how mundane the action, I was delighted.

To my surprise, the euphoria continued Monday. Back we drove to Portland, (happy-happy-happy) flew south to LA, (ho-ho-ho) drove home (hee-hee-glee). The joyfulness train continued chugging through Tuesday and Wednesday. And while it lessened slightly, I remained present in a pleasing state. I considered yelling at a neighbor but felt too calm.

At different moments while writing, taking out the trash, or in bed at night, I'd think of Eugene: a bird in the trees along the Willamette, a cedar chip running trail, a remark made by another runner, a spectator sign. Serenity and peace continued to enfold me. Could Heaven be thus?

Finally, on Thursday, something angered me, ending a phenomenal stretch. I never told anyone about it, not even Joy. Like sex, the sensation can be described via metaphor, but the experience is beyond language.

As the new year commenced, I pondered those post-Eugene days. All that neuromodulator was released after only seven months of training. What kind of endocannabinoid cascade might be triggered after finishing a marathon following years of struggle? Interesting thought. Still, I didn't add a marathon to my 2021 athletic calendar. In fact, my goals were quite modest:

Run consistent with excellent chi running form.

Postpone the Mesa 10K.

Lose another 30 pounds

Run a 10k by July

Run 10 miles by December

Immediately, I achieved goal number two. Because of a COVID Delta variant outbreak, Mesa canceled their 10k. Strike one off the list.

Enmeshed in publishing complications, my exercise remained limited. I walked in early January, stationary cycled, then ventured a few runs later in the month. Some soreness lingered in the knee tendons and ligaments. Stationary cycling helped reduce the ache.

A bit more running in February, increasing to thrice a week. Plenty of cycling and core work. By March, I'd completed e-book and softcover versions of my short story collection and experienced a surge in physical ambition. As the *Ever Given* cargo ship blocked the Suez Canal, I accepted the loss of the Mesa race. Then I signed Joy and me up for a July 5k.

Because of the Delta variant, the LA Marathon had been postponed to the fall. I recalled a rainy night, a house in the hills, and a vow to run LA. I decided that if July's 5k finish time were under 35 minutes, I'd train for the LA Marathon. I doubted I'd even reach the start line. Something always seemed to happen.

To become faster, you need to run faster. Mondays became speed day. I would run for two minutes, gradually building up to a fast pace, then holding it until my timer beeped. After resting a minute, I would repeat. Each week I'd add another repetition. Wednesdays became long run days—3 miles beginning in March. Fridays were tempo runs—fast miles in the middle of a run. Saturday or Sunday, I'd pedal on my stationary bike.

Musing about Eugene had benefits beyond nostalgia. I realized I'd lost mental toughness. The absence of mental toughness could be measured in the number of unfinished writing projects, my weight, and my foolish injuries.

Digging around our bookshelves, I found *Running Within* by Jerry Lynch and Warren Scott. Written in '99, this book on body-mind-spirit performance had helped me train for Phoenix. During the Eugene run-up, I'd reread certain parts. The authors offered methods to harness the power of affirmations and visualizations. Here are a few notes I made:

Prepare your body by raising the fitness floor.

Train the mind by practicing pushing just outside your comfort zone.

Remove decisions—fatigue increases effort—inclined to take easier routes—reduce the choices you must make.

Have a big reason—accountability—use race for something bigger.

I knew the value of visualizations. My current training reacquired a mental component. I dusted off my fuchsia 3x5 card. Underneath the 5:29:59, I marked four lines for 5k, 10k, half-marathon, and marathon finishing times—should I ever again approach 26.2. I also crafted a little jingle for running hills:

Mr. Hill,
Yes, you will,

Make me strong,
Tough and chilled.

It kept me occupied fighting gravity.

Four-mile-long runs returned in May. Wanting to test my speed, I signed up for a TNT virtual 5k. On a Friday morning, I dropped by the Rose Bowl. Pasadena motorcycle cops were busy training in Lot K, weaving around traffic cones.

I wanted to finish in 34 minutes and 20 seconds. For a change, I set my running app to measure kilometers. Flush with new mantras, I bounded off past motorcycling cops, passing a scattering of other runners and walkers. Nature blessed my efforts with a marine layer. One Rose Bowl lap later, I logged a 33:41. Very encouraging. I felt confident about breaking 35 minutes at the 5k.

At home, I chewed over matters running. At some recent point, I'd changed. Subtle fears nagged me like salesmen at a health club. I now worried that no injuries would arise and I'd have to run the marathon.

An alien mythic event, marathons seemed ominous. I struggled to check negative thoughts. *What if I set a time goal and choked? What if I miss a cut-off point?* I saw myself bonking in a Sea of Humanity race, caught on a thousand cell phone cameras, and my pathetic collapse flashed around the Web as a punchline. I'd lost all conviction in my abilities.

Collapse point.

I fought the dark mental thoughts. Okay. Running a marathon again scared me. *Do you even want to? Yes. Who will even know? Joy and I. Who will care if you don't? I will.*

A few days passed. I ran, wrote stories, took my mother-in-law out to lunch, ate snacks, watched old movies, and flipped through *Running Within*. I thought of Ventura.

It was a nice town with a beautiful old mission church. Wasn't the Surfers Point route a seaside run, flat course, double loop, small field? I imagined there'd be spectators, a horn or two, maybe a few cheerleaders from the local high school, but nothing like teeming LA.

Recalling the library and the 2005 TNT sign-up meeting, I realized it didn't matter which race I chose. In my current state, I'd have problems with any marathon. All that remained was be or do.

The closer a race date, the greater the entry fee. Signing up for a fall marathon in May made sense. But my fingers hesitated over the keyboard. Not since the '08 California International Marathon had I plunked down money for 26.2.

I signed up for Surfers Point.

All that remained was running my July 5k, checking comparative times, then training for four months without injury. When had that happened last?

Still, entering a marathon felt bold, nostalgic, surreal.

Five-mile runs returned in June. I reinstituted run/walks. At first, 3x1. In addition, I began checking my old running logs. Once I passed six miles, I'd be encountering issues of hydration and fueling, especially in hot weather. I'd forgotten so much about distance training.

When the alarm beeped Saturday morning, July 3rd, I didn't want to run. At the Rose Bowl, I didn't want to attempt my goal time of 32:59. Joy hadn't trained but was content to walk the course. Why not walk with her? This year's race would not finish inside the Rose Bowl. Probably some arbitrary COVID restriction. By 8:00 AM, the temperature nudged 80 degrees—Chicago memories. The runners then surged forward.

I started out fast and wanted to quit after fifty yards. Then I slid over to the right-hand side of the course, preparing to walk. Though breathing hard, I wasn't gasping. I felt I could hold the pace. Since I knew the Rose Bowl well, I could chill and focus on my chi running form. For the first mile, runners passed me in bunches. During the second mile, I picked up speed and passed a few people. In the home stretch, a guy sped around me but ran out of gas. I caught him at the finish line. Beyond the mat, a teen handed me a bottle of water and a medal.

31:51.

Joy finished and we rolled to breakfast. I ate the blueberry pancakes of the just. I woke up and left my air-conditioned home. I ran, didn't slow, and beat my goal time by over a minute.

The Surfers Point Marathon was Sunday, November 7th.
That Monday would be July 5th.

On the fuchsia 3x5 card, I filled in the 5k space, then retaped it to my computer.

Marathon training had commenced.

Chapter Fifteen

Old Ground

"Failure is always an option."

– Adam Savage

Surfers Point was on asphalt bike paths.

To better prepare, I transferred the bulk of my running back to Pasadena. A marathon truism recommends training on terrain similar to your upcoming race. The Rose Bowl loop would provide the asphalt. The surrounding hills would toughen me up. To quote Frank Shorter, "Hills are speedwork in disguise." They'd prepared me well for flat Phoenix and net-downhill Eugene.

Around then, Joy's health took a disturbing downturn. From late July into August, her temperature spiked at night, rising into the hundreds. She'd sweat like a fountain, followed by chills as if battling malaria. Returning to normal for a few days, Joy would then repeat the whole cycle.

Because of COVID regulations, health insurance compelled her to Zoom call. If she couldn't get her doctor, she'd have to take the first available physician. One doctor diagnosed her with COVID. Joy and I were tested. No COVID. A second doctor proclaimed her malady as pneumonia. Because of Joy's condition, I canceled a training race in Huntington Beach. Since 2020, this was my third aborted 10k, now the Distance-That-Dare-Not-Be-Run.

As Joy wrestled with her health, I ran eight muggy miles in early August. Long runs were conducted at a constant low to moderate intensity pace. This helped enhance the body's ability to funnel oxygen to the muscles as well as teach the body to burn fat as an energy source. Shorter faster runs aimed to push the system more and prepare me to hold a marathon pace. Checking old training logs, I added another running day, upping my weekly total to four.

Following the eight-mile run, my resting heart rate took off at a gallop. I had trouble sleeping. Those symptoms often indicate stress hormones. It's a sign of overtraining. I rested a week, limiting myself to easy stationary biking. My system rebalanced. That was good, as the following week I would attempt ten miles.

Not since the day I met spitlk had I covered double-digit miles. Ten miles intimidated me. It'd crept up so fast. I'd expected some new health catastrophe would stall my training. But the way ahead was wide open.

In his book *Chi Marathon*, Danny Dreyer writes: "Glycogen, water, and electrolytes are the three things on which your body relies to keep moving. If you run low on fuel, your body will stop running. If you run low on electrolytes, your muscles will stop firing and you'll get muscle cramps. If you run low on hydration, your blood will thicken, and your heart will have to work harder than it already is. You must replace these three things during your long runs and most definitely on race day."

In the late summer heat, I'd need to carry sufficient liquids up into the waterless forest. And since I'd be running for over two hours, my body would need refueling to avoid glycogen depletion. I found an old water belt that held two 20-ounce plastic bottles: one for Gatorade—electrolytes—and the other for water—hydration. Stopping by Run With Us, I grabbed some gu. Gu is both a brand name and a nickname for foil packets of energy paste, like athletic baby food. On a long run, I'd squeeze them into my mouth, replenishing glycogen.

At 7:30 AM on a Wednesday morning, I drove to the Rose Bowl. As Kabul fell to the Taliban, I prepared to run ten miles as if it were 2008 and we'd only been in Afghanistan seven years. Late August conditions were good. With temperatures under 70 degrees, cool ground air was pressed upon by warmer air above, keeping the clouds from dispersing. Along with this marine layer, a light breeze puffed across the arroyo. Wearing my double water belt, I sloshed north from Lot K, running three minutes, walking one. I headed two miles north, crossed under the 210 Freeway, and up a steep rocky hill.

The rocky hill proved a chore. Other than an outlier or two, for years I'd been covering a few miles every week on rolling terrain. Now it was time to test chi running on rougher ground and longer distances. Through the tunnel under Oak Grove Drive, then out the other side to Devil's Gate Dam.

Beyond the dam, the flood plain was undergoing a three-year plan to remove excess sediment and restore natural habitat. Trucks of all sizes and shapes idled, rumbled, and beeped. I ran past busy men in colorful vests and helmets.

Past JPL, up another steep hill, I crossed the triangular bridge—four miles from Lot K. Before me lay ground long untrodden. Sharing the rocky paths with hikers and mountain bikers, I angled up into the Angeles National Forest. A mile later, I rounded a bend in the trail and slowed at the Elmer Smith Bridge. How weather-worn the old sign had become. I could barely read the words. Nonetheless, I slapped metal, ate a gu, then started back down.

Over the last two miles, a thin misting rain fell. My feet burned. I suspected worn padding. I'd need new running shoes.

2:12:03.

Cooling down around the Rose Bowl I bumped into Van, M.I.T Dave, and Esther. They met every Wednesday morning for a three-mile stroll. I told them I was training for a marathon but mixed-up Surfers Point with Surf City. Southern California lacked nothing if not races with "surf" in the title. They wished me well and I bounded off, feeling spry and energetic.

Awash in heady sensations, I drove home. The chi running form had held up over distance, integrating well with run/walks. I'd stayed hydrated and felt no glycogen dip. According to my training schedule, I'd run another ten miles next Wednesday. After that, the distance would really ramp up, culminating in a 21-mile run. Then the mileage would descend to Sunday, November 7th.

Two weeks later during a 14-miler, my shorts fell off.

Not all the way. I grabbed them just in time. A stocky runner weaved around me, watching the spectacle of a man in his late 60s clutching running shorts with one hand and a water belt with the other.

"How's it going?" I asked.

He turned away, perhaps uttering a prayer that death would claim him before elderly haplessness.

I blamed my two twenty-ounce bottles. Stopping to tighten the belt, I mused that I was nearing run's end. I'd already drunk most of the liquids. Shouldn't my shorts have fallen off at mile one with both bottles full? Odd. Well, I was tired and not thinking straight.

I returned to running over rolling terrain, dirt trails, then downhill onto the blacktop. My shorts kept inching below the water belt. On the last mile, I picked up the pace. Reaching the pedestrian track surrounding the Rose Bowl. I approached runners and walkers moving in the opposite direction. They eyed me curiously.

Held high, my right arm was swinging naturally, elbow floating back, fingers cupped lightly as if holding a dandelion. Meanwhile, my left arm gripped the waistband of my shorts with the desperation of a one-armed man dangling from a bridge.

At the northwest corner of lot K, I crossed my finish line. I wobbled, uncomfortable. The soles of my feet burned as if I'd been firewalking. My nipples were sore.

Waistband firmly in hand, I crossed the road to my jeep. For a while, I sat behind the wheel, recalling another September and an oak tree with wide leafy branches. Now even its stump was covered by asphalt.

I chuckled.

Having dropped 30 pounds since January, my weight loss was showing. What bothered me were sore nipples. Run far enough and repetitive friction between flesh and shirt would cause a man's nipples to bleed. Blood on your shirt made finish line photos appear gross and freakish.

Later back home, I discovered an old pack of nip-guards. Comparable to round Band-Aids with foam rubber padding and adhesive, I'd purchased a pack for the California International Marathon. They fit over my nipples, keeping them from chafing. From now on, nip guards were left out on Tuesday nights with my other long-run gear.

I figured the foot burning was a shoe issue. My old Brooks trainers had soles thick enough to stroll on bubbling steel. But the padding had worn down. I bought a light, comfortable pair of Sketchers.

A step-back week arrived where training eased off and my body grew stronger. Wearing the new shoes, I ran a leisurely eight miles, the second half at 4x1 r/w. Doubts arose. The Sketchers seemed light; their soles too thin. I also thought the toe box lacked room for swelling.

Back to Run With Us where they were delighted to see me again. I bought shoes with thicker soles. The new Hokas felt excessively padded. I was keenly aware that my training was speeding by. Pardon the phrasing, but I was running out of long runs. Race day shoes needed forty to fifty miles of break-in to loosen up. If Hokas weren't THE marathon shoe, I'd need to find the right pair fast.

With a 16-miler approaching, I reviewed 14. It wasn't a stellar run. A fire had closed the Angeles National Forest depriving me of my eight and ten-mile markers and forcing route improvisation. Rushing out the door on a hot morning, I hadn't brought enough salt tabs or gu. On the back end of the run, my energy crashed like a cement truck driven by chimps. And my feet still burned. My whole running style had changed since 2008. With chi running, I landed differently. Was it really the shoes?

That Friday I cracked the 10k jinx. Returning to Griffith Park, I set my phone's running app to measure kilometers. Then I ran a 10k in my new Hokas. Overall time for 6.2 miles seemed excellent for a man breaking 5:30:00. In fact, my finishing time indicated I might even manage a 5:11:00 marathon. Wouldn't that be sweet? I added the 10k time of 1:09:15 to the fuchsia 3x5 card.

Joy's health improved. She'd finally booked an appointment with her own doctor. He ordered her to the clinic for tests. Imagine that? A doctor who still performed tests. As it turned out, all summer Joy had been fighting an exceptionally nasty strain of urinary tract infection. The right antibiotics finally knocked it down. It was good seeing my wife enjoy a little decent health after a miserable summer.

Post-16 miles, my feet once again burned. Plus, my chi running form fell apart over the last four miles. One crisis at a time. YouTube burning feet suggestions ranged from lacing my shoes too tight, to wearing thin socks, to employing excessive body glide lubricant to my soles. Perhaps I was unused to long runs on asphalt.

All those years pining for a marathon and now it was down to weeks. Next Wednesday was 18 miles, then a practice half-marathon, then 21 miles, followed by a three-week taper to the race. I considered postponing the marathon but that was nerves talking. I needed to figure out this hot foot issue.

The Squid Game was quite popular. I'm not a big series guy, but this one hooked me. As broke Koreans died on-screen by the platoon, I ran a mapping expedition for my 21-mile run.

The Arroyo Seco Canal trails begin a mile south of Lot K. Wearing new double-ply socks, I loped beneath the mundane 134 Freeway, underneath the death-shrouded Colorado Street Bridge, descending finally toward a cluster of stables in South Pasadena. As horses snorted and clopped in their corrals, I marked three miles, then reversed course back up to Lot K.

For 21, I figured to head south to the stables and back for six miles, then three around the Rose Bowl for 9, a mile down and back to the start of the Arroyo Seco trail for 11, then 10 miles up to Elmer and back for 21. Hopefully, the fires would be under control by then and the forest trails back in play.

After flirting with a faster marathon time, I recommitted to 5:29:59. *Don't change anything now.* Eighteen miles hurled toward me. For the last six miles, I planned an increased run/walk to 5x1 at marathon pace.

Another Wednesday, another long run. Because of the late September heat, I arrived at the Rose Bowl around 5:30 AM. Still dark, you could see runners and cyclists, their headlamps bobbing like lost miners. Down in the arroyo, the temperature stood ten degrees cooler, chilly. I wished for gloves.

Mid-morning, I was back in my jeep eating gummy bears and chugging water. I considered replacement marathons for Surfers Point. Santa Clarita was also in

November. I'd run my first half-marathon there in '05. But too soon. The Mesa Marathon took place in February. Maybe.

Replaying events, I was glad the Angeles Forest had reopened. However, my 18-mile run had stunk. Marathon pace for the last six miles? Ha! In the latter miles my feet burned, though not as bad as previously. Hydration, glycogen, and fuel schedules were upended. Going out too fast, I was underhydrated, missed two gu sessions, and hit the Wall like a moth flying into a bug zapper. For the last four miles, I could barely lift my feet. Almost toppling, I staggered across the Lot K finish line, frightening a female jogger. At least my shorts didn't fall.

Back home I showered and returned to bed, sleeping several hours. Sitting down to work that afternoon, I shifted the cursor around but wrote nothing worth keeping. At dinner that night, I barely tasted the food. Lacing my shoes correctly wasn't the issue. But what was the issue?

And what had happened to cross-training? I'd logged no stationary cycling for weeks. I needed to regroup from my sloppy training. My feet still burned. It was almost October.

I needed more time.

Chapter Sixteen

By a Thread

"The marathon is a competition between your will and your possibilities."

— Jeff Galloway

After years of struggle, injury, illness, and operations, the marathon had arrived like a tardy fireman, long after the house had burned. With dozens of little distance-running balls in the air, I felt overwhelmed. Friends of mine used to say, "Seriously, I could never run distance. Too boring." Oh, really?

Pressure built. The race was in charge, dragging me forward by the shirt front. I hadn't even booked a Ventura hotel room.

On the Web, mental toughness strategies are legion. They are as numerous as schemes for congress to enrich itself. Alongside *Running Within*, I'd been experimenting with various methods, including *10-Minute Toughness* by Jason Selk.

Here's a sample chat with a friend:

Me: My feet burn when I run more than fourteen miles.

Friend: How come?

Me: I don't know.

The first rule of Fight Club is don't talk about Fight Club. Selk's rule for discovering solutions is similar. Now imagine the above conversation whereby I substitute a friend for Jason Selk.

Me: My feet burn when I run more than fourteen miles.

Selk: Why?

Me: I don't know.

Selk: The first step in figuring out the "I don't know" is to stop saying "I don't know."

Me: What happened to my friend, Selk? Where is he?

Following a post-18-mile funk, I battled a desire to quit the marathon. *Pull the plug. Go ahead.*

I dug deep and focused.

Project Hot Foot needed a solution in two weeks. I played Selk's game. Shoes, lacing of same, socks, body lube, and insoles all seemed unlikely culprits. So why were my feet burning? I don't—now I squirmed. The next logical step was a chi running form review.

Notes from chi running classes, the chi running book, YouTube videos, and DVDs were all studied. I even bought the e-book version of Danny Dreyer's *Chi Marathon* (with Katherine Dreyer). Seeking clues on where I went astray, I gleaned several useful ideas, especially on watering and nutrition.

But nothing on the burning feet.

At the same time, I discovered Doctor Alan Goldberg. A sports performance consultant, Goldberg's YouTube videos were short, concise, and practical. He addressed the psychological impact of everything from injuries and lack of confidence to slumps, practice, and superior performance. He'd supply simple exercises for returning a wandering mind to the task at hand. (Goldberg called the mental wandering "time traveling.") From Goldberg, I deduced that finishing time should not be a distance runner's focus. He should concentrate on the individual elements making up his form. Finishing time would take care of itself. Fortunately for me, chi running was positively swamped with form elements.

Tension built up like deep ocean swells before the wind.

As the training half-marathon approached, I crafted a race plan. I'd run 21 kilometers around the Rose Bowl for maximum asphalt acclimation. My guing would commence at six miles and continue every twenty minutes. I'd also pop a salt tablet at six miles. Every ten minutes I'd swallow a mouthful of water and monitor my chi running form. No run/walks. No emphasis on time. Form, form, stinking form.

Another cold pre-dawn Wednesday morning.

Down in the arroyo, a cyclist passed me as I loosened up. LED headlamp gleaming, the man had attached a five-foot, fluorescent orange pole onto the rear of his bike. Here was a cyclist announcing his presence to all. Then away into the gloom he sped, his orange pole waving side-to-side like the tail of a fluorescent dog.

First light colored the eastern sky. That morning I'd experimented with breakfast, a meal I normally skip. I'd munched a banana and drank a sixteen-ounce water. Better learn now how my system reacted to food prior to long runs. Cuing up my running app, I activated the Ironman interval timer and set out.

As the sun rose, the Rose Bowl crowd thickened. Maintaining my watering, form-checking, gu-eating timetable, I noticed a young woman approaching. In terms of speed, she resembled Coach Kate but without the light tread. The woman slapped her feet as if killing silverfish. *WHAPWHAPWHAPWHAP.* I could hear her approaching fifty yards off. But, man, she was fast.

Keeping a steady pace, I dispersed tension in my shoulders and neck. Watering and guing continued on schedule. Some runners passed me huffing and puffing. A few approaching runners would wave or nod. Old men walked four across, blocking the pedestrian loop, forcing runners out into the road where the spandex-clad cyclists lurked.

Women strolled in twos and threes and fours, with or without strollers. A few skaters glided around the swelling crowd.

Early morning now and a diagonal line of geese flew over Lot K, honking like Armenians in a parking lot. Around ten miles (16.1 kilometers), soreness grew in my glutes and IT bands. Not bad, but they would surely worsen the longer I ran. I made a mental note to check my chi running literature on possible causes. If something hurt, my form was off.

And then there was one more lap. A slight tenderness crossed the soles of my feet. Ahead in the crowd, I heard a faint *whapwhapwhapwhap* as I crossed the finish line.

2:39:26.

At last, a decent run. I'd finished with energy, well-hydrated. During the run, I'd initiated form corrections, something I hadn't been doing. Form focus had been key and not the clock. Most important, the run was a monster morale boost.

Back home that morning, I added the half marathon time to the 3x5 card.

Only one more line remained empty.

But Project Hot Foot still required answers. Since I could no longer say "I don't know," I pressed on with chi form research. At the same time, I planned next week's 21-miler as if the issue were still shoes. At the eleven-mile mark, I'd pass my jeep. There I'd refresh with water and Gatorade for the second half. And I'd change my shoes. I even considered icing a fresh pair of socks. This gives you some idea of my desperation.

I'd ordered a pair of Brooks Ghost IIs. They would be THE marathon shoe. But the new footwear wouldn't arrive before the last of the heavy mileage. I'd need to wear the Ghost IIs on every taper run just to break them in.

Traditionally, the twenty-miler was the last training hurdle. Afterwards, you'd taper, decrease mileage, and let your body recover from the hard pounding. (October would be my second hundred-mile month in a row.) According to a paper published in the *International Journal of Sports Science*, muscle glycogen and enzymes increased during taper. Back in the day, I recalled a growing excitement as race day approached. Holding oneself back during taper was a normal caution.

The Tuesday before 21 was dark with uncertainty. Still no answers to Project Hot Foot. In my office, I sat at the computer and brooded, angry, feet dangling over the edge of self-pity.

Watching an old YouTube chi running video, I spotted something, a possible discrepancy in my form. I recalled 2019 and the self-inflicted pain I'd endured from adding force. In chi running, the angle of your lean determines how high your heels rise behind you. From the video, it appeared I'd, once again, grafted a little muscle onto the movement, lifting feet without the proper lean, then dropping them down behind me. Not much, a tiny amount of effort. But that tiny amount happened 170 times a minute; 10,200 times an hour for several hours. Hot foot. Could it be that simple?

In the arroyo the next morning, a gibbous moon shone cold and aloof in the west.

Once again, I loosened up before the first light. Temperatures were parked in the low 40s and I'd forgotten gloves again. I did bring a warm sweater. For the first time during training, I needed to urinate pre-run.

In deserted Lot K, I experimented with my form, practicing short surges, and focusing on lean. I had a lot of ground to cover that day. After walking a half mile to warm up, I set my interval to 5x1. Adjusting my metronome to 170 beats per minute, I fell forward.

First light cut the eastern sky like a knife through silk. I ran along the Arroyo Seco Channel, under the rumbling 134 Freeway, beneath the haunted Colorado Street Bridge. I wouldn't know until the second half of the run if my corrections worked. In the meantime, I stayed loose, focusing on form, and watching my step on the rocky trails.

South three miles to the stables and turn around. On my way back, I noticed four people and five dogs on the opposite side of the canal. A coyote yipped from a hill above me. ("Hey, dogs, I'm going to eat you.")

The dogs barked back. ("Na-huh. No way. We're with humans.")

Back up to Lot K, then once around the Rose Bowl. Dawn dialed up the sunlight and the morning crowd was gathering. Two geese on the nearby golf course engaged in a honk-off, back and forth, each daring the other to quit.

Early morning as I finished my loop and monitored my lean, taking care not to add any muscle to my heel lift. Watching the ground ahead, I imagined it sweeping my feet back like a treadmill. A two-mile run down and back to the Arroyo Seco trail head gave me 11 miles. I crossed the street to my jeep.

Last week's half-marathon had been solid preparation. So far, I'd run steady, watered, Gatoraded, and commenced the guing process. Now I refilled both fluid bottles, dropped off my sweater, and changed shoes. Setting aside my 2019 Brooks, I now wore the billowy Hokas. The whole changing of shoes had a superstitious feel, like throwing salt over my shoulder. I only wished the Ghost IIs had arrived.

As I headed north toward Elmer, the Rose Bowl loop was filling up. Behind me, I listened but no *whapwhap-whapwhap*. Maybe she was caught in traffic.

Under the Oak Grove tunnel and past the Devil's Gate Dam; into the flood plain and around the many trucks. An older woman walked a huge mastiff. I called out, "That's either a very large dog or a very small dinosaur."

"It's a horse," she said. I wasn't entirely sure she was kidding.

Beyond JPL, up the second steep hill. So far, my feet were holding up. Beyond the triangular bridge, the trail to Elmer grew rocky and narrow at points. A small dog yipped ahead. To my surprise, here came Boston CJ running downhill, holding the critter's leash.

Having also shifted training back to our old trails, CJ inquired about Ernesto. Sadly, after many years, Ernesto and I had ceased our Saturday breakfasts. Lockdowns claimed our favorite coffee shop. Work and family kept him occupied most weekends. We'd met once the previous year, long before I'd signed up for Surfers Point. CJ wished me luck on the long run, and we parted, certain to meet again.

My feet were hot, but not burning. I sensed the Hokas had nothing to do with it. Rounding a bend in the trail, I slapped the Elmer sign. It felt excellent.

Five miles left. I'd been drinking more water than usual. Washing down gu with Gatorade left me feeling over-sugared, mouth sweet and cloying. For the last two miles, I dropped the run/walks and picked up the pace.

4:43:52.

I hadn't run that long since pre-Eugene.

Cooling down afterwards, I recapped the run: a subtle correction had carried me the 21 miles. Feet were somewhat warm, but the burning was lessened. Hydration and guing had gone smoothly. My toes felt bruised. These Hokas were good shoes, but not roomy enough for marathon swelling. I needed the larger Ghost IIs.

Back home, showered and coffeed, I did a little math. That morning's finishing time averaged out to around 13.5 minutes per mile, one minute above my expected marathon pace. That was fine. Considering the hills and the trail conditions, I should be able to nail my 5:29:59 splits on a flat course.

Opening a new tab on my computer, I booked a hotel room in Ventura.

Chapter Seventeen

Starting Block

"There is no terror in the bang, only in the anticipation of it."

— Alfred Hitchcock

F our days before the race, I couldn't sleep.

Every training mistake I'd made returned and brought friends. During the day, I'd be listening to Alan Goldberg videos and thinking positive. At night, negative thoughts would burst in. They'd beat up the positive thoughts and trash my confidence like looters inside a Louis Vuitton store.

That Saturday, Joy would drive us out to Ventura. On Sunday, whatever the outcome, Joy would drive us back to our hotel. Until then, I planned on watching more

Goldberg videos, trying to visualize perfect chi running form.

As marathon plans go, mine was simple: maintain pace. Don't exceed it by more than five minutes. Assess at the half-way point. In the later miles, don't wait for the finish line to scurry forward and meet you. From Mile 22, relax and finish strong. I printed out a pace band with splits at 12:35 per minute.

On Thursday, I cleared the guest bed in my office and laid out all my gear. Surfers Point was a Mom-and-Pop event, lacking massive booth-rich expositions like the Sea of Humanity races. In Chicago, you could walk into the exposition cold and buy everything you needed for the marathon. In Ventura, I'd pick up my runner's packet at a strip mall bike shop.

On the guest bed were nip-guards, body glide, gu, water belt and a pair of twenty-ounce plastic bottles, shirt, shorts, bib with my race number and a chip inside, a man diaper for my incontinence, hat, sunglasses, sunblock, salt tablets, Ghost II shoes with 48 miles of wear, double-ply socks, handkerchief, eye drops for my lenses, a small kit for lancing blisters, pace band, metronome, Ironman sports watch with the interval set for 5x1, a small towel, sweat pants, light jacket, and carpet slippers for before and after.

This ritual display of gear erased the last unreality of the marathon. The rocket was on the gantry. All I needed to do was stay centered. But serenity wasn't coming easy.

I wrote on Friday, then tried to relax with a book but couldn't concentrate. I napped and hoped to wake up and find the marathon had passed. For dinner, I ordered a pizza.

Suddenly, it was Saturday and time to go. Antsy, I wanted to criticize Joy for the speed she drove and the route she took to Ventura. Mercifully, I shut up and twisted my hands.

After picking up my race packet at the bike shop, we ate lunch, then checked into our hotel. Everything seemed slightly imperfect, somewhat off, unsatisfactory. Stupid employees wearing stupid COVID masks had closed the stupid breakfast buffet, and I wasn't even going to be around for breakfast. Jumpy, I unpacked.

In the evening, we attended Mass at Saint Buenaventura, an ornate old church and the last of the nine missions founded by Father Junipero Serra in 1782. Ventura was also home to Erle Stanley Gardner, author, lawyer, and creator of the once-popular attorney Perry Mason. There's a plaque in town commemorating Gardner, who also dedicated time and talent advocating for those screwed over by the legal profession.

Afterwards, we dodged roaming homeless men and went to dinner. Joy and I ate at a Mexican-themed restaurant. Judging from the surrounding table talk, the eatery had drawn other runners for tomorrow's event. Back in our room, I laid out all my gear on the spare bed. For breakfast, I set out a banana and a sixteen-ounce bottle of water. That would last me until guing commenced at the 10k mark.

Marathon gun time was 7:00 AM. I set the alarm for 5:00 AM. Joy and I discussed our race day plans. As Carl von Clausewitz once remarked, "The enemy of a good plan is the dream of a perfect plan." In other words, keep it simple. Here was the support scheme: Our hotel was only a few minutes' drive from the start line at Emma Wood State Beach. Joy would drop me off, then scoot back to the room and crash. We'd meet again at the marathon halfway point. I'd finish the first half between 9:35 and 9:45 AM. Then Joy would top off my fluids. Afterwards, she'd split once more, returning as I crossed the finish line at 12:30 PM.

I lay in bed that night with the negative chorus chittering away. *You didn't train enough. Your knee will crack like a rotten board. You're too old for this distance and a jerk for even trying. Your feet are too big. You're gonna choke on the back end and miss your goal by three seconds.*

Glancing at the portable alarm clock, I wondered if I would fall asleep at all. In Honolulu that happened, where I'd dropped off, only to wake up almost immediately. Tonight would be the start of Daylight Savings Time. Fortunate me. I'd gained an extra hour of uneasy wakefulness. I'd probably want to stay in bed the next morning. But I usually felt that way pre-race.

At some point, I dozed.

Beep-beep, beep-beep, beep-beep.

With Joy still asleep, I quickly silenced the alarm. In the bathroom, I began the process of body gliding all the relevant parts: soles, heels, in-between the toes, crotch, nipples. The spitlk, surgeries, depression, pain, frustrations, quitting, starts and restarts, and stupid me-caused injuries were gone like a stone dropped into a deep pool.

There was only now.

Joy was up a little before 6:00. I'd added a cup of coffee to my breakfast banana and water. Wearing my race bib, carrying my gear check bag containing Ghost IIs, pacing the room in carpet slippers, I kept checking the time.

Then we headed for the door. We paused for a prayer. Nothing fancy. No age group records or television interviews. I asked God for the strength to not quit that day. My weight was down to 220 from 260 back in January. I'd trained to the best of my ability. For the first time that year, I felt I'd done all I could.

A murky cool morning greeted us.

For once, I'd remembered gloves. At the Emma Wood State Beach North Campground, I waved bye to Joy. All around, tents and booths were still being erected. A gray chilly day boded well—excellent distance running weather. Hopefully, the marine layer would hold until early afternoon. I wandered around, visited a Porta-Potty, and noticed few runners. A tunnel under nearby train tracks led to the beach. I considered watching the surf roll in. Instead, I loosened up my joints.

For the next thirty-five minutes, time crawled like a line at the Department of Motor Vehicles. A runner jogged past, warming up. More and more runners arrived. The minutes sped up. I dropped one of my water bottles. By now the start/finish line inflatable arch had been erected. The timing mat was laid out. A line had formed near gear check.

Sitting atop a picnic table, I removed the carpet slippers. On went the Ghost IIs. Gloves, sweatpants, slippers, and jacket were stuffed into the gear check bag. Carrying the twin-bottle water belt, I handed my bag to the gear check guy. Since the race ended where it started, my clothes would be waiting when I finished.

Hereitishereitishereitis.

Runners with blue bibs were lining up. Toward the back of a very sparse marathon pack, I took up position and secured my water belt. Surfers Point water stations would feature a novel device. Instead of being handed a cup by volunteers, runners would foot-pump liquid into their containers. How very COVID. I knew my twin bottles would carry me through the first half.

Marathoners wore blue bibs, half-marathoners red, 10k runners green, and 5k yellow. A quick look around indicated a marathon field of around a hundred runners. Quite intimate. Since this race was billed as a Boston qualifier, they'd be very speedy runners.

In my two-bottle belt, with a pace band around my wrist, I appeared Mr. Retro. Most of my blue-bib peers toyed with smartphones. I deliberately hadn't brought a smartphone, saving me lost time on selfies and landscape videos.

A short middle-aged woman in a yellow watch cap asked, "Is this a wave start?"

"Yes. The half marathon starts fifteen minutes after us, then the 10K, then the 5k."

A fellow blue bib, Yellow Watch Cap seemed disappointed by my answer, as if she'd bet money against a wave start.

I shook one leg, then the other leg. Reaching up, I fiddled with the sunglasses atop my cap. I glanced at my Ironman. Almost ten after 7:00. *What are they waiting for? Celebrities?*

Coated in clear packing tape, the ends of my pace band were held together with a safety pin. My right wrist was slick with body glide in anticipation of pace band friction. I exhaled loudly. *Cheap little race. Just start any old time. Because they're out in the sticks, they don't care. I should've run LA. They'd start on time.*

Ahead of me, runners darted under the inflatable arch.

Leaning forward at the ankles, I hit my cadence metronome, then the interval timer on my Ironman.

Beyond the timing mat, I crossed into race land.

Chapter Eighteen

Loop One

"Experience is one thing you can't get for nothing."

— Oscar Wilde

The course followed a bike path uphill for a mile and a half. Yellow Watch Cap ran behind me, talking to a male runner.

"For the first five miles, I don't mind if I'm last in the race."

"It's the later miles, right?"

"Right," she agreed. "That's when I take off."

After five minutes, my watch beeped. Moving to the right of the course, I let Yellow Watch Cap pass as I took my first walk break. A minute later, a second beep signaled time to run. A few runners flashed me quizzical looks. ("Don't quit now.") I knew these early walk breaks would pay off down the stretch.

A bridge spanned a tidal pool. This was the turnaround point for the 5k race. The blue bibs continued past. From atop the bridge, I saw rows of orange traffic cones, marking the course to the northwest. The view was beautiful. Off to the right, east beyond two-lane Pacific Coast Highway, the ground rose to train tracks, then up again to four-lane Highway 101. Gradually, the rising earth became the gray rock and green scrub slopes of the Santa Ynez Mountains.

Descending the bridge, I glanced west at the slate-colored Santa Barbara Channel. Surfers in wet suits bobbed on the swells, awaiting the right wave. The surf rumbled and broke against Solimar Beach.

I had a small insight: this was a loop course. Five miles ahead was the turnaround point. Then back the same way to Emma Wood. Then out again. Consequently, my first and second loops would require uphill runs to the bridge. The second loop would occur during the dog miles of the marathon. *Too early. Don't even think about it.*

A young trio of blue bibbers passed me, laughing, two men and a woman—friends entering a marathon together. To my surprise, a red bibber zipped by. Then a few more half-marathon pack leaders. I sped up like a motorist caught daydreaming in the fast lane. *Run your race. Focus on form.* I throttled back.

A blue-bib couple in their early thirties ran around me. The man was tall, the woman a bit squarish and short. Quite the gentleman, the man hustled forward to a water station, operated the odd pumping device, and returned to his companion with a water container. I guessed he was her marathon Sherpa. For many subsequent miles, The Couple would be my unofficial running buddies.

Inland from the beach, jumbled boulders stretched toward a group of distant houses. Seagulls found the boulders a perfect hangout. A few crows mingled in for the sake of diversity, but most of the birds were raucous chattering seagulls. Hopping to the asphalt, they'd steal trash from each other or tussle over scraps. I was reminded of a Hollywood business meeting.

A gull flew north at chest level, just missing me. Above the road, a wire extended across Pacific Coast Highway. It attached to a pole near the boulders. Seagulls lined the wire like soldiers at a communal john. I swerved around large white splotches splattered on the asphalt like some avian Rorschach test.

I was near the back of the marathon. Around me, red bibs passed. Then a few of the front-running green bibs.

Nearing the end of the boulders, I approached the Solimar Beach Colony, a collection of multi-million-dollar homes. Racing through residential neighborhoods in Eugene, people in their yards would shout encouragement. At the Sea of Humanity events, someone was always boosting your spirits.

But no Solimar colony dwellers sat outside in lawn chairs with signs saying, "Go Runners," "You Can Do It," "Almost There." Other than an occasional "looking strong" from a water station attendant, Surfers Point appeared to be a runners-only marathon. Not that it mattered then. I was still basking in my early-race glow.

Beyond the colony was Mondos Beach. It featured the same rocky boulder line as Solimar. Supposedly Mondos was a good spot for novice surfers and longboarders. After a westward jog, Faria Beach lay ahead, another colony of seven-figure homes. A county park lurked within its posh confines. At the front gate, a cop minded traffic so runners would not be flattened by speeding wealthy.

Passing Pitas Point, the course continued northwest. Ahead stretched Rincon Parkway Campground. From Pitas Point to the turnaround several miles ahead were a line of RVs. The big vehicles seemed stretched out to infinity, or, at least, Oregon.

I'd read that you could see the Channel Islands from Rincon. I wouldn't know. All I saw were Class A, B, or C vehicles: Winnebago, Liberty Coach, Phoenix Cruiser, Roadtrek, Gulf Stream Coach, Jayco. RV people were out early and wishing everyone a good race. Occasionally, there'd be an empty parking space. Running past one such vacancy, I spied a rock cairn piled up Zen style. Some RV Buddhist had parked, enjoyed oneness, then split.

From behind, red bibs passed me to the right and left, bound for the turnaround at the end of Rincon Beach.

Meanwhile, blue bibs ran toward me, passing on the right and left as they streamed back toward Pitas Point. The green-bib turnaround had been on Solimar Beach, otherwise they would've passed me too.

Fast and slow runners inhabit different worlds. But here we were all smooshed together. It shouldn't have mattered, but I found it distracting. It was like being a pedestrian in the middle of a stock car race. In other marathons, I'd fallen in with people running the same pace. Sometimes you'd talk, but mostly you'd be aware of each other for long stretches. It was comforting, like being surrounded by family members you were ignoring. Here, all I had were The Couple.

At that moment, they'd stopped for a restroom break, leaving me to take the lead. Just then, running felt good. I sensed I was over pace. I made a mental note to dial it down. Focusing on good form kept my mind occupied.

Up ahead, I spotted the water station marking the turnaround point. The water station attendants said, "Hi." I responded in kind as I reversed course. Now it was time to run 6.55 miles back to the start line, completing loop one.

I'd been watering every ten minutes. Now I gu'd for the first time. Fingers sticky from the sugary substance, I wiped them on my shorts. Overhead, the marine layer still held. Checking my pace band against the Ironman, I saw I was six minutes ahead of goal pace. *Not bad. A minute too much. Don't get crazy.*

Returning alongside the RVs, bracketed by red and blue bibbed runners, my Ironman beeped. Time to walk. Walk periods were averaging between thirty and forty-five seconds. A burst of energy raced through me like a tidal surge. I wanted to yell, "I'm doing a marathon for the first time in thirteen years! Do you understand what it's taken me to get here?"

I stayed mute. When my watch beeped, I ran.

At Pitas Point, the course jogged east, then continued southeast.

Passing the gate at the Faria Beach Colony, I noticed a middle-aged cop sitting in his car. The cop was probably assigned this cupcake job because he was approaching retirement. We stared at each other for several seconds, each daring the other to wave. Neither of us broke.

With Mondos Beach to my right, I continued in-between the colonies. As the grade sloped up, I slowed. Music sounded from behind, a pop tune with a female vocal. The Couple passed, digging their tunes.

Back on Solimar Beach, I noticed more surfers arriving, unloading boards from vehicles, or changing into wetsuits. Near the gull rocks, blue bibs pounded toward me on their second loop. In ones and twos, they shot past, most without comment. A few smiled and held up an encouraging thumb or forefinger. One or two said, "Good job" or "Keep going." One guy sported a big smirk that seemed to say, "I'm not you, old man, who will finish hours behind speedy me. I'm not like you at all." I later heard this same man caught an STD.

As the terrain rose toward the bridge, a runner passed. His gait was unbalanced, slightly favoring the left leg. Of blue or red-bib lineage, I couldn't say. I mentally wished him well as the sun finally broke through. *Well, here we go, stinking high temperatures for the second half of the race.* I lowered my sunglasses. But forty yards later, the sun crept back behind the clouds like me returning to bed on weekend afternoons.

Over the tidal creek, then down the bridge. At last, there were spectators lining the route. In marathons past, the time from the midpoint up to twenty were the golden miles. You beamed confidence, on pace or ahead, goal as good as reached. Approaching a hill, I felt unease. I wished I'd signed up for the half-marathon.

Good old Emma Wood lay dead ahead. More spectators roamed the sides of the course, looking for loved ones. Bemedaled finishers walked about with friends. Teenaged-girl volunteers in electric yellow T-shirts cheered us on. Beyond the finish line, runners milled around, enjoying beer and tacos as upbeat music boomed. Such merriment!

At the end of the finisher's chute, red, green, and yellow bibs passed beneath the inflatable arch and across the timing mat. Their race was run. Blue bibbers pulled a hairpin turn to commence the second loop. Naturally, the lead marathoners were already enjoying their second round of beer and tacos.

I spotted the finish line clock: 2:33. Not good. I should've been arriving closer to 2:45. There's a marathon fallacy called "banking minutes." It goes something like this: Run faster than your pace in the first half. Then, in the second half, you've banked the necessary minutes to sustain you through the Wall. I didn't believe it, but I was behaving as if I did.

Spotting Joy, I stepped off the course. Together, we topped off my water and Gatorade.

"How's it going?" she asked.

"A little ahead of schedule, but I'm feeling good." I swallowed another salt tablet. "Come back around 12:30."

"You're gonna beat this thing."

"Thanks. I own this nasty-ass race."

Out once more past the Electric Yellow Teenagers and up a hill. The festive finish line sounds faded behind me.

Uneasy thoughts returned. *Too fast, too fast. You're gonna bonk.* I batted them aside. *Focus on form. Release all tension.*

As I approached the bridge, my mental tennis match continued.

Chapter Nineteen

Loop Two

"But he that dares not grasp the thorn Should never crave the rose."

— Anne Bronte

Downhill to Solimar Beach.

An older red-bib couple ambled up toward the bridge. In no time, they'd be face deep in beer and tacos. Lucky stiffs. A few blue bibs sped past Emma Wood bound. I recognized several runners as they'd passed me four times that morning.

At the next walk break, I bunched up my shoulders, then released them, easing tension in my upper back and neck. Burning flared up in my feet, but not bad. One of the laughing trio of young blue bibs from loop one trotted ahead. Separated from his two amigos, he glanced at a smartphone screen, then angled toward a water station as if following directions. From the beach, gulls cried, and the surf rumbled. Out on the channel, surfers bobbed, black forms like caraway seeds on an immense watery bagel.

Up ahead I observed The Couple. In good spirits, they'd since dialed down the music and were chatting. I considered hanging behind them. At least I'd be near runners going at around my pace. For a time, I played a game, attempting to define their relationship by body language. I settled on co-workers.

She'd heard him in the breakroom talking about his past marathons and implored him to be her Sherpa. But the guy was engaged and didn't want friction with his fiancée. The female co-worker was desperate to complete a marathon because other women in the office teased her about her weight and lack of athletic ability. She'd even followed the guy on a date, hoping to catch his fiancée in the Ladies' Room and ask if she minded. But the fiancée misunderstood. The women quarreled. The fiancée and the guy split up.

Nearing the Solimar Beach Colony, I sped up and passed The Couple. I figured they'd leapfrog me later and I could finish this running romantic comedy.

Nothing new on race day is an old marathon adage. No new shoes, socks, gels, hat, nothing you haven't used in training. You're reducing the possibility of an unpleasant surprise by vetting everything within your control. As Mondos Beach and the Faria Colony fell behind me, I entered something new on race day: running solo. I'd expected to train alone and run my 21 miles with no encouragement. But I wasn't prepared today for Rincon Parkway.

Unlike the late miles in Phoenix, there was no Coach Kate beside me. As the course turned northwest at Pitas Point, the red bibs were gone. A few blue bibs loped past, but for the most part, I ran alone. No rock 'n' roll "Born to Run" or "Eye of the Tiger," or "Running Down a Dream." No steel bands playing "Brazil," taiko drumming, high school cheerleaders, runners dressed as Ninja Turtles, bulky pace groups, friendly crowds, yelling kids, water stations overstaffed with volunteers, or Japanese men in wooden clogs. No clusters of running grapes. Even the RV people seemed to have moved back inside for a second breakfast. I'd taken for granted the distracting utility of such things. Around me were gray sky, asphalt, and the line of RVs stretching into infinity like Hell for people who hated RVs.

Seventeen miles and the negative thoughts oozed in.

Walk longer. Give yourself a break.

A blue-bibbed dude in his twenties approached. Sporting a dark goatee, the man wore a cardinal and gold USC shirt. As an alum, I flashed him the school's two-fingered Fight On sign.

"Fight on," he smiled as we passed.

That rare little human moment helped.

In fact, go ahead and walk now.

Late morning arrived, and many RVs were leaving. Huge vehicles lunged onto Pacific Coast Highway like elephants departing a water hole. Up ahead I watched an RV man lose control of his dog. The animal ran into the road and across the street, leash dragging behind. Crossing to the embankment, it turned and trotted back toward the RVs, pausing in the road to bark at oncoming traffic. The man gave chase. However, the dog scuttled under a different RV. Pursuing, the man almost snagged the leash, but the dog darted under yet another RV. With the outcome still in doubt, I ran past.

Several empty RV spaces provided a view of Rincon beach. A rump beach if there ever was one, probably underwater at high tide, Rincon was also lined with boulders. If the Channel Islands pined to be seen, I wasn't looking.

Up ahead, I spotted the turnaround point water station. The crew seemed tired, having hailed their quota of runners for the day. As I doubled back along Rincon, they managed a courtesy wave. Parts of my body were beginning to ache. I was already sick of gu. But if I stopped now, my energy would crash sooner than need be.

I tried to cheer myself up. *Next stop: finish line.*

It's a rising grade from here on. Better rest. Don't kill yourself.

Passing the RVs once again proved a tricky distraction. When pulling out, not every driver noticed a slow runner. Comparing my Ironman to wristband, I was seven minutes over pace. Time to go full Goldberg. *Focus on form, water and gu on schedule, release tension.*

I grew obsessive over 20 miles. I searched for signs that I'd hit twenty. Banners hung along the course listing the miles, but the wind often twisted them into unreadable shapes.

I recited the names of passing RVs. Liberty, Phoenix Cruiser, Jayco. Somewhere in the middle of RV Hell, I passed 20 miles. I don't recall why it mattered. Muddled actions often mark the Wall, the meeting spot of fatigue and reduced cognitive ability.

A surprise: here came The Couple running toward me. Where had they gone? Passing, we exchanged waves. They looked too fresh. Pitas Point fell behind. The course jogged east, then continued southeast. Ahead lay the colonies, then the bridge, then the blessed inflatable arch.

Back off. Forget surging at mile 22. You aren't going to finish running. Ease up now or you'll buckle and beg that Faria Colony cop to drive you back.

A young cycling couple zoomed past.

"How much further?" said the woman.

"Five miles."

"Good luck. Get there soon."

"Doing my best, thanks."

Now the Wall was upon me. As stated, glycogen is a carbohydrate used for energy. It's our ready fuel when exercising and the reason I ate all that treacly gu. Nevertheless, my glycogen stores were depleted. I was burning fat. My brain began shutting down. Negative thoughts multiplied like rats in a subway.

Just say you walked in to save your knee. That's a perfectly understandable reason. Anyone who hears that will sympathize.

At Faria Beach Colony, there was a patrol car, but I didn't see the old cop. Then Mondos Beach dropped behind for the final time. Blood pooled in my legs. Like mold spores in a dark warm basement, the negative thoughts grew.

You deserve the rest. Look how far you've come. Could any of your friends do this? Take a victory walk.

Past the Solimar Beach Colony, I slowed to a scuffle. From the impressive pain below my waist, I knew I wouldn't run/walk anymore. Be or do; run or quit.

Walking is best. And you won't be far off your pace. Not at all. It's better this way.

Back on Solimar Beach, I noticed a sign I'd previously missed: Tsunami Inundation Zone. The sign displayed a figure running upwards toward high ground. Where was the tsunami now to end my suffering?

Ahead, I spotted a runner in his thirties, moving slow. Injured? I thought so. In silence, I passed him. He was a fellow blue bib. Up ahead, I searched for a spot where I could walk.

Call it a day. You did all you could.

The temptation to walk scampered through my mind like a burning squirrel. Spying a trash dumpster, I sped up until I reached it. Then eased off.

Orange cones ahead marked the course. I picked up the pace. Passing the cones, I eased off.

Twenty yards further on, a surfboard leaned against the back of an SUV. I leaned my body forward from the ankles, increasing speed, passing the vehicle. Then I slowed.

Around mile 24, I neared the tidal flat bridge. Checking the Ironman, I was startled. My time buffer had dissolved. To my blood-starved brain, it appeared I'd miss 5:29:59. The last line on the fuchsia 3x5 card would scream failure forever.

Comeoncomeoncomeon.

Picking up the pace, I looked out to sea. I stared at the surfers, at the traffic, at a train passing on the railroad tracks. I looked everywhere except at the grade leading up to the bridge. Compared to the hills above the Rose Bowl, this elevation was a bunny hill. But my legs were trashed.

Mr. Hill,

Yes, you will . . .

Yellow Watch Cap ran downhill and past me. This was she of the I-shine-in-the-latter-miles. For whatever reason, the woman was only now commencing her final loop. We passed in silence.

I crested the bridge over the tidal pool. Now back down toward Emma Wood. No spectators this time. A few runners with medals were visible. I aimed at little goals: pass the light pole, pass the guy with the dog, pass the spray-painted message on the asphalt reading, "Bikers suck."

Walking is nice and fun. Clever people walk. You're liked by others if you walk.

Out crept the sun, as if embarrassed at being late for work.

Mile 25.

My form decayed, feet pronated, standing up straight, no lean. I was very close to shuffling, Ghost IIs dragging across the ground like chains behind a tanker truck.

But I could sense the finish line.

Down a hill, then up another one. Lo, the Emma Wood State Beach North Campground. So quiet now. So unfestive.

Mile 26.

From the grass beside the bike trail, Joy took cell phone pictures.

"You're a champion."

I tried to say something clever. Nothing emerged from my mouth but carbon dioxide.

Mile .2

Only a pair of Electric-Yellow Teens remained to cheer. Both sat on rocks texting as I passed. Ahead lay the finishers chute, funneling me toward the inflatable arch. A loudspeaker crackled. A man's voice said something cheery and upbeat. A few spectators applauded my approach like golf fans approving a tap-in putt. Waving back, the smile on my face grew.

Before me stood the arch.

Then I was across the timing mat and beyond.

Normally, Electric-Yellow Teens dispensed finishing medals. None were closer than .2 miles. A race official intercepted me. In his early thirties, wearing horn-rimmed glasses, he held a marathon finishers medal and a plastic water bottle.

"Congratulations." He tried handing me the items. Too blood-starved to think, I acted out of instinct, bowing my head. Surprised, Horn-rimmed Glasses dropped the water bottle and hung the medal around my neck.

"Congratulations," he said again—an actor doing a second unwanted take. Crouching to retrieve the bottle, I almost toppled.

Light-headed, I weaved around the finish line area like a stoned bee. The beer and taco stands were closed. The crowds had gone. I thought again of walking to the sea. This time I'd stand in the cold surf, letting the ocean soothe my aching legs.

Instead, I found the nearest curb and collapsed like a marionette, waiting for Joy to find me.

Chapter Twenty

Cool Down

"A minute's success pays the failure of years."

— Robert Browning

Installed three years before the Lakefront 10 Miler, our stove lacked a functioning clock or timer. Meat could emerge fully cooked or exotically different. Culinary outcomes were more art than science.

Joy hankered to cook a turkey that Christmas. So, we measured the space in the kitchen, then visited several stores. After mulling over various stove candidates, we selected a new convection oven. Christmas was a week off as we settled in for a quiet holiday.

But with a turkey parked in the refrigerator, Joy got sick again. It was something bronchial involving copious coughing and hacking. Then a sinus bug smacked me. I sneezed like a maniac. Being incontinent, every sneeze carried with it a liquid discharge, a "sneeze tax." Once more, my apnea and a stuffy nose meant little sleep. On the new glass-topped stove, Joy and I cooked mostly soups.

As we recovered from our maladies, I assembled thirteen years of blog posts, training logs, race plans, and journal entries. In addition, I gathered up scraps of paper, scribblings on the back of race bibs, and old coaching-tip emails. For example, here are some notes I jotted down post-Surfers Point:

Miles I wished I'd run the half-marathon: 11, 13.1,14, 17, 22.

Miles I wanted to fake a knee injury so I could stop: 23.

Miles I wondered what people would say if I just quit: 22 and 23.

Miles where I couldn't walk and didn't want to run: 21, 22, 23, and part of 24.

No endocannabinoid avalanche followed Surfers Point. (I was hoping it would.) The night of the marathon, cramping calves kept me awake, thrashing like a hooked carp. After breakfast the next morning at Denny's, we drove home. I yawned, serene and satisfied like an old dog in the sun. The whole experience seemed fantastic, like owning a car that always stalled until the day it carried you coast-to-coast without pause.

On the fourth line of the fuchsia 3x5 card, I wrote in 5:22:49, then put the card away.

"Often, I do not know toward what I am running. Most of the time, I do not care. I cannot precisely see my goal, but I can talk about getting there."

Hal Higdon's marathon reflections resonated. So, what was my overarching goal? It sure wasn't praise. I'd pulled away from social media. Less than ten people congratulated me on finishing Surfers Point. Besides, no amount of Likes could compensate for the training and the race itself.

It might've been as simple as something friend Karen once wrote about understanding happiness and seeking it out.

Or finishing what you started. I've had problems with that. Spitlk killed off one dream. But I learned that failure can be less harmful than complacency. Gradually, I'd forged a new dream and followed its corkscrew twists and pivots to the end.

Still, I thought there would be more and it would be obvious. An epiphany; a bonus life lesson grand enough for thirteen years. But the race ended, and time's tide surged over the moment.

As physiologist and coach Jack Daniels once said, "Injuries are the savior of runners." A bittersweet blessing, to be sure. But several running friends no longer run. They walk or cycle or sport artificial hips and knees. But I still zip along on stock limbs, thanks to all the rest and recovery thrust upon me. In their own annoying way, spitlk and the operations and injuries extended my athletic shelf life.

I'm one who'd rather curse the darkness than light a candle. Often, I allow an all-or-nothing mentality to dominate. If I couldn't get what I wanted, my life sucked when it didn't. Then I would wallow in self-pity. As the last marathon fades, I try to employ various mental-toughness techniques to fend off negative thoughts in every aspect of life. Today, I'm willing to consider taking the candle and matches out of the drawer while cursing.

"Often, I do not know toward what I am running."

But I always know what I am running from.

Over the course of chasing the marathon, my marriage went from troubled to worse. The collapse of our careers, money woes, stress, and anxiety over health issues generated pressures that dogged Joy and me for years. When I was healthy, marital tension was easy to dodge. Go out for a run and feel good. Avoid the stress. With running removed, I was compelled to face unpleasant matters. To stay afloat, Joy and I were forced to communicate and work together. Painfully, over years, we reconciled our hurts and flaws. In time, we became a team.

There are no medals for that marathon.

On the back nine of life, our finances are stable and our health—up and down at times—is basically good. Thanks to chi running, I'll keep logging the miles. I might even venture another marathon. But if not, I'll retire the distance with honor.

As for the marathon, I still don't know what I was running toward.

But now you know how I got there.

The End

Acknowledgments

"Time moves in one direction, memory in another."

— William Gibson

Thanks to all the many participants, coaches, team and mission captains, honored teammates, and campaign managers I encountered during my years with Team in Training, San Gabriel Valley Marathon Team, Greater Los Angeles Chapter. I learned a great deal about running, surrounded by optimistic, upbeat people out to challenge themselves physically as well as help those suffering from leukemia and lymphoma. Go team!

As always, my veteran beta readers Ken Segall and Dan Hoffman provided insights into my sometimes esoteric copy. In addition, valuable input was provided by TNT veterans Van and Virginia Garner, Jimmy Dean Freeman, and Kate Martini-Freeman. Their insights helped make an okay book better. Coach Kiley Akers battles lung cancer but found the time to read this manuscript. Just know that Kiley is determined to recover. His heart remains set on once again roaming the ultramarathon trails.

Proofreading services were rendered by Wonderlist. Once again, Brandi Doane McCann—no relation—of EBook Cover Designs performed as her work title suggests and designed the cover art.

And finally, thanks to my wife, Joy McCann, who always corrects some little thing I'd never even consider. Any errors are the result of me insisting matters go my way.

Resources

Here I present several of the running techniques as well as the psychological methods referenced in the book. I received no money for promoting these sites and it wounds me.

- Chi Running

- Jeff Galloway Run/Walk

- Global Cycling Network

- Jason Selk

- Dr. Alan Goldberg

- *Running Within*

About the Author

An Emmy-winning TV animation writer, JP Mac lives in the hills above Los Angeles, He and his wife Joy enjoy long walks and Indian gaming. Mac is working on a series of thriller novellas plus his first fantasy novel. A life-long runner, he is considering another marathon. For now, Mac scares off the coyotes by jangling his running medals. Say 'hi' at:

a amazon.com/JP-Mac/e/B00H7R0A8Q/ref=aufs_dp_mata_dsk

g goodreads.com/author/show/7535682.J_P_Mac

in linkedin.com/in/john-p-mccann-379ab47/

v twitter.com/JPMacauthor

Or visit his website: JP Mac@Squarespace.com
And, of course, stop by the obligatory mailing list where freebies, discounts and notifications on Mac's latest works may be found. Go to: https://tinyurl.com/ycm d7p8z

Also By JP Mac

Fiction

Death Honk: Nine Tales of the Macabre

Hallow Mass

Fifty Shades of Zane Grey

The Little Book of Big Enlightenment

Nonfiction

They Took My Prostate: Cancer-Loss-Hope

Jury Doody

About the Publisher

This book is indie-published. Reviews matter very much in keeping our small business going. If you enjoyed this book, please review it on Amazon, Goodreads and anywhere else you choose. Even a single sentence will help our visibility.

Should you elect to review this book in print, or for a website, blog, vlog,or podcast please let us know so we may highlight your views on social media.

— Joy McCann
Production Manager
Joy.mccann@gmail.com
Cornerstone Media

La Cañada,
California

Made in the USA
Las Vegas, NV
05 September 2022

54728903R00125